creating

HISTORY

DOCUMENTARIES

a step-by-step guide to video projects in the classroom

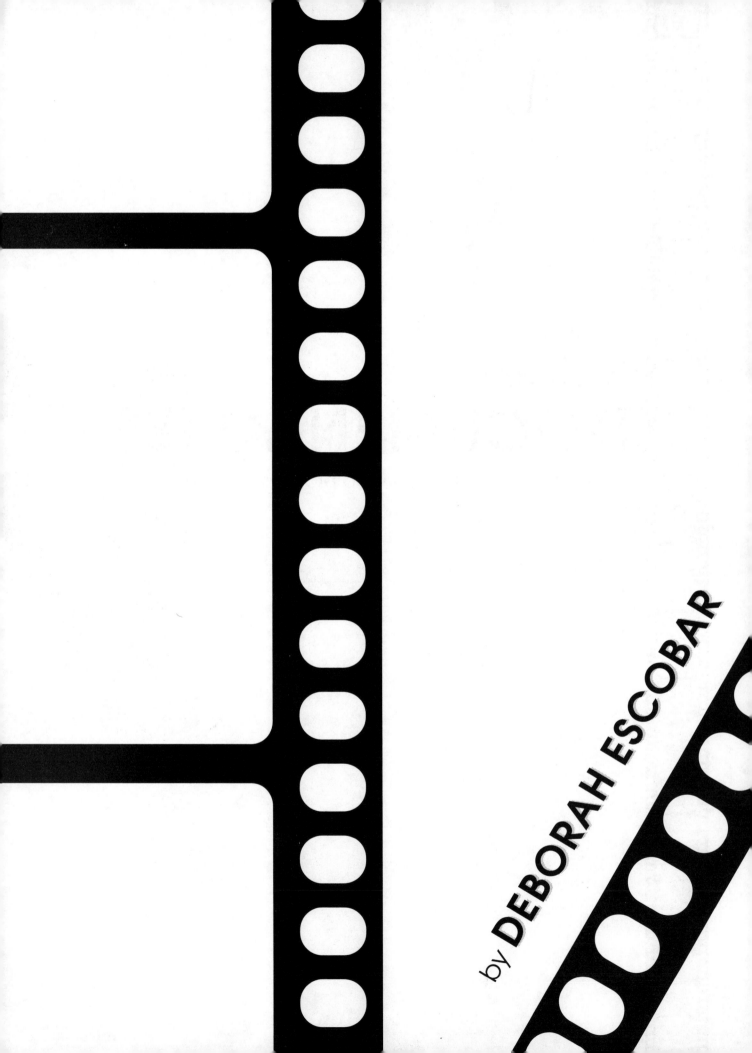

by **DEBORAH ESCOBAR**

creating HISTORY DOCU-MENTARIES

a step-by-step guide to video projects in the classroom

PRUFROCK **P**RESS **I**NC

Printed in the United States of America.

ISBN 1-882664-74-4

Prufrock Press, Inc.
P.O. Box 8813
Waco, Texas 76714-8813
(800) 998-2208
Fax (800) 240-0333
http://www.prufrock.com

Table of Contents

Worksheets and Forms

Introduction

This student handbook was created in order to assist students as they produce their own history documentary. Students sometimes get lost in the research process, spending huge amounts of time on one type of research or getting bogged down on learning one of the technical skills required. A step-by-step process, with a targeted timeline, allows the teacher to keep track of student progress while "scaffolding" the project into small chunks. Students who are supported in this way are more likely to be successful in completing a documentary.

System requirements differ according to the graphics card and software you use (see the section on Technology Support), but minimal hardware and software needs are:

- minimum 166-MHz Pentium MMX (266-MHz Pentium II recommended) or equivalent;
- a minimum of 32 megabytes of RAM (64 MB recommended);
- at least one gigabyte of free hard drive space for program and work space, with an additional 100 megabytes of storage for each project;
- a video card with 2 megabytes of video RAM, minimum 800 x 600 resolution at 16-bit hi-color (65,000 colors). Direct Draw Drivers recommended. (ATI All-in-Wonder, Dazzle are two examples of video cards). Video cards capture analog, digital, or both;

- 16-bit stereo sound card and speakers;
- monitor (17-inch recommended);
- CD-ROM or DVD-ROM drive;
- editing software (examples include MGI's VideoWave III, Ulead System's VideoStudio, etc.);
- VCR/TV setup and connection cables (usually provided with graphics card);
- camcorder (digital camcorder optional);
- scanner;
- photo imaging software (Adobe Photoshop, for example);
- Internet access; and
- digital camera (optional).

For those who do not have access to desktop editing hardware/software, ideas on linear editing techniques are also included. Creating a history documentary is a lengthy project. For extracurricular projects, the timeline targets that are provided allow for five months of independent study, with frequent teacher-student conferencing on progress. Time spent on research can be adapted to classroom needs with the suggestions provided, but realize that the quantity of time available for research directly relates to the quality of the end product.

To the Teacher

I won't fool you—being a facilitator for students as they complete a history documentary is not an easy thing to do, especially when working with desktop video editing for the first time. It takes an adventurous but patient soul to begin incorporating new technology into the curriculum. Please realize that there is a tremendous learning curve that goes along with any new technology being used; but, once the apex of that curve is reached, you will find that the benefits to your teaching are well worth the time it took to learn the process.

When I first began working with small groups of gifted/talented students on history documentaries, we were limited to in-camera editing, assemble editing, or photographic slides. I was pleased with the student research, yet the process of creating a presentation was frustrating and the quality of the product often suffered. When computerized slideshows like Microsoft's Powerpoint and Corel's Presentations came on the market, I was eager to incorporate the new technology and found that the professional quality of the product greatly increased student interest and motivation. At that time, the process of using these slideshow programs was thought by many to be too time-consuming to be adaptable to the regular classroom. Surprisingly though, within two or three years, a number of teachers had adapted computerized slideshow projects for full classroom use. It seemed that, as soon as a few teachers took the time to become familiar with the technology, they passed on their knowledge to others who found it to be a worthwhile teaching tool. I predict the same thing will happen with desktop video editing.

Meeting National Social Studies Standards

The creation of a documentary enriches student understanding of history because they are actively constructing their own view of the past. The historical inquiry they undertake promotes in-depth study and develops historical perspective. As students analyze primary sources, compare and contrast evidence, and search for causes and effects of events, they are applying knowledge in a meaningful way—not because they are given an assignment, but because they begin to love historical thinking. Students enjoy the "real-world" feel of creating their own documentary, especially when they are told that it is exactly the type of work professional historians accomplish. If they are then given the chance to show their work to an appreciative audience—in a contest like National History Day or to parents, a historical society, another classroom, or even perhaps an airing on a local public access television channel—they gain in self-confidence and academic pride.

This documentary project is closely aligned to standards that have been adopted by the National Council for the Social Studies, and specifically meets Standard No. 2: "Time, Continuity, and Change":

- Students will learn to understand their historical roots, developing a historical perspective by reconstructing the past through study of primary sources.
- Students will learn to apply key concepts such as time, chronology, causality, change, conflict, and complexity.
- Students will use critical-thinking skills to explain, analyze, and show connections between patterns of historical change and continuity.
- Students will interpret the past by searching for causes and effects tied into historical events.
- Students will learn to check credibility of sources, evaluate for bias, and assess multiple perspectives.
- Students will gain an appreciation of differences in historical and/or cultural perspectives and will recognize that societal values and cultural traditions influence how events are perceived.

■ Students will develop an understanding of change over time and be able to relate historical events to present issues and public policy.

This project also meets the Historical Thinking Standards that have been adopted by the National Center for History in the Schools, specifically those of historical comprehension, analysis, and interpretation. Other social studies standards will be met dependent upon the topic or era chosen for the documentary.

The project can also be tied into standards in other disciplines. Language arts standards can be met through reading of sources, note taking, writing and revising of a script, and public speaking (recording) of the narration and/or presentation to an audience. Math can be used in the evaluation of sources, creation of a survey, analysis of statistics, graphing, and so forth. It is easy to see how technology standards would be addressed by scanning, digital photography, and digital editing involved in such a project. Depending on the subject matter of the documentary, science standards can also be incorporated, as in the case of students who did an in-depth investigation of the Love Canal toxic waste disaster.

Working With Students

The history documentary unit is flexible enough to be tailored to your classroom or curricular needs. The project can be integrated into a social studies class curriculum or used as an interdisciplinary unit as a graded cooperative group activity. In this regard, it is especially useful for honors social studies classes. The project could also be used with gifted/talented students as a pull-out or enrichment cluster course, or as an independent study that is offered to above-average students as an enrichment challenge. The project easily forms the basis for an extracurricular history club, with the goal of entering completed product(s) in National History Day or similar competitions.

The following suggestions for structuring history documentary projects can be adapted to time constraints and curricular needs. It is suggested that students be assigned into cooperative groups, with four to six students in each group (Note: For National History Day competition, group size is limited to five students.)

Tips for Cooperative Learning

- Groups should be heterogeneous, with a mix of ability level, interest, talent, and gender.
- Each group member should be specifically accountable in each phase of the project. All students should be responsible for note taking and background research. A handout of suggested group roles during research is located in Step 1. Suggested group roles during production is located in Step 10.
- Assessment should be a mix of individual and group grading. It is suggested that the project be graded at several different intervals to give students feedback about their progress. For example, grades could be given for completion of note taking on background research, in-depth investigation of primary sources, draft and/or finished script, and finished product.

Adapting the Project for Use in the Social Studies Classroom

Elements of a Good Documentary—One Class

Introduce the project by showing a 10 to 15-minute clip from a professional documentary and having students fill in the "Elements of a Documentary" worksheet. You may want to have your school's media expert visit as a guest who can discuss these elements with students. Go over group roles and expectations.

Step 1: Topic Selection—One Class

Topic selection can be inquiry-based, but you can design the parameters and allow students to choose topics within your curriculum needs. You may wish to provide students with a list of possible topics, investigating resources that are available in your school's library ahead of time. Whenever possible, think of angles to tie curriculum ideas into local historical topics. You may find that students do not think local topics are interesting because they fail to think from the specific focus to a general historical trend, concept, or issue. Encourage students to make those connections by incorporating one of the following ideas:

- "book-talk" or "picture-talk" that gives background on how a local historical topic relates to national or international historical themes or issues;
- "show-and-tell" assembly or after-school event at which local war veterans or senior citizens share their experiences with students;
- "walking tour" of a local historical neighborhood or field trip to a historical site;
- field trip to a local historical society or archive, during which students can view some of the materials available for research; or
- historical archives or organizations often provide speakers who bring slides or other presentations into schools.

Assign groups to read Step 1 of the handbook, complete brainstorming, and choose a topic by the next class. They should also be asked to bring a file system or three-ring binder to the next class.

Step 2: Bibliography and Project Management—One Class

Pass out three to five copies of each different type of bibliography form to groups, along with the page on "How to Do an Annotated Bibliography" and the example of a page of a bibliography. Go over each form, making sure students understand how to fill in the information correctly. Discuss note-taking guidelines and how to focus a topic, using the handouts provided. Have students complete keyword brainstorm and explain procedures that are used in your school for keyword searches of the library catalogue. If your school has computerized search capabilities, use the handout on search strategy that is provided.

Step 3: Background Research—Three to Five Classes (Over One or Two Weeks)

Bring students to the school library and let them begin research and note taking using encyclopedias or other general reference works. Ask them to use the school library catalogue to find and sign out books on their topic. Assign them to take notes, emphasizing the need to develop a timeline of events. (Note: You may want to have books reserved and kept in the library if you have multiple groups working on the same topic(s) or time period(s). If this is the case, you will probably want to provide additional class or study hall time for use of these sources.)

Step 4: In-Depth Research and Primary Sources—Two to Five Classes (Over Two to Five Weeks)

Using handouts in this section, make sure students understand the difference between a primary and secondary source. Additional research time will be needed to find primary sources and analyze them. Have students complete the "Research Leads Worksheet" using information gathered from their background research and the bibliographies provided in secondary books. You may want to give students an assignment to complete a written analysis, using the questions provided. To make it easier for you to assess whether they understand how to analyze a source, you could provide the same primary source document to all students and check their analyses.

You can shorten the time needed for in-depth research by providing students with collections of primary source documents for their topic or time era. Collections of primary source documents are available for purchase from a variety of vendors, including:

- Jackdaw Publications, P.O. Box 503, Amawalk, NY, 10501. Variety of primary source packets that feature high-quality reproductions.
- Cobblestone Publishing, 30 Grove St, Ste. C, Peterborough, NH 03458; (800) 821-0115. Print reproductions of various primary source documents, organized by topic.
- Primary source publications are available from the National Archives and Records Administration at a very reasonable cost. Two volumes of *Teaching With Documents* ($15 each) include a collection of about 100 primary documents and give suggestions for classroom use. Other specialized packages are based on the Bill of Rights, Constitution, and westward migration. Information on how to order publications can be found on their web site, along with suggestions for teachers and worksheets/activities that help students analyze different types of

primary sources (see example). Go to http://www.nara.gov and click on "Digital Classroom."

The site also allows for keyword search and retrieval of the thousands of primary source documents that have been digitized by the National Archives and Records Administration. From the home page, go to "Research Room" and click on "NAIL database." In addition, NARA also provides a free one-hour electronic workshop for classes of up to 30 students in grades 5–12. The school would need to have ISDN-based videoconferencing capability. For more information and technical requirements, go to http://www.nara.gov/education/professional/vcinfo.html.

- The American Library of Congress has an excellent collection of primary source documents (including movies) online in their American Memory Collection. The site also gives access to lesson plans and activities for using primary sources in the classroom. Go to http://memory.loc.gov/ammemo, enter the site, and click on "Learning Page."

There are many CD-ROM collections of primary source documents, including:

- *American History: Resource Links* ($116.95), a set of four CD-ROMs that allows users to create their own slideshows or multimedia presentations using the primary source materials provided. Available through the Social Studies School Service, http://www.socialstudies.com, or call (800) 421-4246 in the U.S. and Canada, or (310) 839-2436 internationally.
- *American Journey 1896–1945* ($34.95), featuring 1,300 printable photographs, maps, charts, and text and over two hours of original speeches, radio broadcasts, and eye-witness accounts. Published by Ibis Communications, Inc., 9350-F Snowden River Parkway, Ste. 251, Columbia, MD 21045; (800) 938-1101.
- The definitive collection of primary source video is a 42-volume laser disc collection titled *Video Encyclopedia of the 20th Century*. It is in use at thousands of schools and universities within the United States. If your school does not have this collection, call area colleges or universities.

Written Document Analysis Worksheet

1. Type of document (Check one):

____ Newspaper   ____ Letter   ____ Patent
____ Memorandum   ____ Map   ____ Telegram
____ Press release   ____ Report   ____ Advertisement
____ Congressional record ____ Census report   ____ Other

2. Unique physical qualities of the document (Check one or more):

____ Interesting letterhead   ____ Handwritten   ____ Typed
____ Seals   ____ Notation   ____ "Received" stamp
____ Other

3. Date(s) of document:_____

4. Author (or creator) of document: _____

   Position (Title): _____

5. For what audience was the document written? _____

_____

_____

6. Document information (There are many possible ways to answer A–E.)

   A. List three things the author said that you think are important:

_____

_____

_____

B. Why do you think this document was written?

_____

_____

_____

C. What evidence in the document helps you know why it was written? Quote from the document.

_____

_____

_____

D. List two things the document tells you about life in the United States at the time it was written:

_____

_____

_____

E. Write a question to the author that is left unanswered by the document:

_____

_____

_____

Designed and developed by the Education Staff, National Archives and Records Administration, Washington, DC 20408. Example of one of the Document Analysis Worksheets available at http://www.nara.gov.

If you prefer to have students do their own research, consider arranging a field trip to a local or state archival facility or library. Use the information provided in Step 4 to make sure that students understand proper procedure for working in a historical archive. If it is possible for you to do an advance "scouting" trip on your own, it helps to set up the experience. When I bring my students to the New York State Archives, we make a full day of the experience and use the New York State Library, which is located within the same building. I divide students (I get another teacher or teacher's assistant to help supervise) and rotate the experience with half in the library, half in the archives.

On my scouting visit, I order carts full of books on the various research topics to be waiting for us on our field trip date. I also talk to the archivists and have documents and collections pulled (when they relate to the topic). Archivists may want to give a short talk to students to make sure they understand correct procedures and handling of documents. Advance legwork assures me that the field trip will be a positive, hands-on research experience.

Steps 5–9: One Class Period a Week (Over Two to Four Weeks)

Divide these steps among the participants in the group, according to the cooperative research roles that have been suggested in Step 1. Class time allows for coordination between group members and check of progress by teacher. Schedule research time if possible. Have students complete the "Progress Check" worksheet (see Step 9) at midpoint and conclusion of research.

Step 10: Write Script—Introduce (One Class) and Provide Group Time (As Needed Over One to Three Weeks)

Explain the handout on change in group roles for production, making sure that students are chosen for each role. Length of class time required for this phase will vary, depending on meeting time that is available for groups. Begin by discussing what makes a good introduction/conclusion and how to develop a topic point-by-point or chronologically.

Give the outline as a graded assignment with a specific due date. This is the step where students may need some extra coaching or encouragement to get started. It is useful to schedule camera time for students once an introduction has been successfully written. This "action step" will generate increased motivation to complete the product.

Step 11: Storyboarding Script—Class Time as Needed (Over Two Weeks)

Writer(s) now have the assignment of filling in the script with detail, statistics, and quotations. This should be a graded assignment with a specific due date. Allow for writing conferences with teacher and group members. If students have difficulty with this part of the process, suggest they approach it as if they were writing a report on what they have learned.

When the script has been completed, make enough copies of the storyboard so that each group can have at least a dozen. Provide time for group work in this phase of the project, either during class or before or after school. This is one of the most time-consuming and tedious parts of the process, so check on students frequently to ensure that they remain on task.

Step 12: Filming (Over One to Two Weeks)

Give this work as an assignment to be completed out of class, but make sure students understand the techniques for camera work. You may need to make arrangements to have a camcorder available after school for those students who do not have one at home.

Step 13: Editing and Production of Documentary— Introduction (One Class) Plus Computer Time as Needed for Each Group (Over Two or Three Weeks)

Give a mini-workshop or demonstration on using the editing software, making sure that students are familiar with aspects of the software pertinent to their group role. Print out "help" sections within the software or pages from software handbook as needed.

Step 14: Writing of Bibliography/Process Paper
(Homework Assignment Over One Week)

For assessment, the student self-assessment forms can easily be adapted for use by the teacher.

Adapting the Project for Use as an Interdisciplinary Unit

In approaching fellow faculty members about the possibility of creating an interdisciplinary unit, it is important to stress the advantages such a project would have for fulfilling standards requirements in the other disciplines. All teachers feel the strain of trying to "manage the curriculum." It sometimes seems that we are asked to incorporate more learning objectives than ever in less time.

The move toward block scheduling has helped to ease this problem by providing additional time for research projects and interdisciplinary teaching efforts. Regardless of your school's schedule, a project like this will require shared planning time, and that will most likely require funding. You may wish to look into the possibility of creating this unit as a summer curriculum project if funding can be found through your school district or state education department. Other possible sources of funding might include:

- state archives or education department grants for record management or educational use of documents;
- university or college education departments may be able to guide you to funding sources;
- state or local teachers' centers often have a library that includes information on grants, and sometimes have small grants available if teachers are willing to conduct an in-service class after the unit has been created; and
- state or local history associations may be interested in sponsoring this type of curriculum development.

Ideas for incorporating into other disciplines include:

- *Technology.* Technology standards in your state may include curriculum on photography (camcorder and digital camera), scanning, digital photo editing (Adobe Photoshop or other programs). Technology teachers might also be interested in incorporating digital video editing.
- *Math.* At the middle school level, the math curriculum includes graphing and statistics. Math teachers may be interested in working with students on designing a survey and statistically analyzing the results or help with creating or interpreting tables or graphs using statistics that have been found during research.
- *Language Arts.* This project will fit language arts objectives for research, bibliography, and writing of script and process paper. Public speaking objectives may be met through the narration of script and presentation of product to an audience.
- *Science.* A topic list could be prepared that would satisfy science requirements, particularly for learning about environmental issues or inventions.

Adapting the Project for Use With an Extracurricular Club or Independent Study

When working with students on a project like this outside of the confines of the regular classroom, it is important to offer students a motivation for completion. In the best of worlds, we would like to think that students would work hard and complete projects for the pure, intrinsic joy of learning—but we live in reality. In our world, people consistently put the most effort into something that will bring them a tangible reward, and students are no different. For this reason, entry into a history contest like National History Day is the perfect motivator. If you decide to introduce this opportunity to your students, copy and pass out the flyer that follows this page.

When presenting this project as an extracurricular activity, it is important to make sure that parents are notified of the educational benefits the student will receive through completion. Extracurricular projects require the students to spend many hours outside of the school day on research and completion of the product. Consider scheduling a parent/student meeting at which you pass out information on the project and discuss rules of the competition and how parents can assist within the parameters of the contest rules. Show them examples of model projects and answer their questions honestly. Also discuss any entry fees, travel expense, and other costs, as well as what funding can be provided by the school district and whether students will be participating in a fundraiser. You may wish to ask for a parent volunteer to coordinate a fundraiser.

Once students and parents have been informed about your expectations, ask for a commitment from the student. Examples of group and individual learning contracts for extracurricular work are included. Give each student a copy of the timeline and be clear about target dates and requirements for completion. Use time within the club meetings to check on progress. Copy and use the "Step-by-Step Guide" as an independent study handbook for students to read on their own.

Consider scheduling specialized workshops to assist students with building skills. Examples could include workshops like the following: Strategies for Internet Search, Writing a Letter, Camcorder Use, and Editing Software. Members of the community might be willing to volunteer to assist in these workshops. At my school, we had a member of the local historical society (a retired teacher) who was thrilled to come and present a workshop on how to analyze historic photographs.

What is National History Day?

The National History Day program is an exciting way for students to study history and learn about issues, ideas, people and events that are of interest to them. The topic chosen must relate to a yearly theme that is chosen by the National History Day organization. Students express what they have learned about the historical topic through creative and original performances, documentaries, papers, or three-dimensional exhibits.

National History Day is organized at regional, state and national levels in most areas of the U.S. At each level of competition, outstanding achievement may be recognized through certificates, medals, trophies, or monetary awards. The most important rewards, though, are the skills and new knowledge that students gain as they complete a project. Students compete in either the Junior Division (grades 6–8) or Senior Division (grades 9–12) in one of the following contest categories: Paper (Individual Only), Individual Exhibit, Group Exhibit, Individual Performance, Group Performance, Individual Documentary, and Group Documentary. Each category in each division is judged separately. Groups may include two to five students.

In most areas, students bring completed projects to a regional competition that is held in the early spring. At this event, teams of judges examine student products and ask students questions about research and construction of the product. The results of this judging are used to choose students who go on to the state competition. Similar judging occurs at the state level, and students are chosen to go on to the national (and final) competition in June, held at the University of Maryland at College Park. Students moving on to a higher level of competition typically use judges' comments from earlier competitions to refine and edit their product for the next level.

Students who participate in National History Day complete an intensive research project that involves deep, analytical research on primary and secondary history sources, critical thinking and problem solving, and learning technical skills required for their type of product. Some of the skills acquired include note taking, research, oral interview, letter writing, organization, graphic design, camcorder operation, video editing, and scriptwriting. Students also gain confidence and experience in public speaking and presentation to judges. The program fosters academic achievement and intellectual growth and is a perfect project for gifted and talented classes because it gives students an above-grade-level learning experience. In addition, while many educators do not like competitive aspects of the program, the competing nature does motivate students to do their best. Exposure to entries at the regional, state and national competitions "models" excellence and teaches by example. For more information, visit http://www.NationalHistoryDay.org.

Lastly, make sure that the students complete the self-assessments in Steps 9 and 14 so that they are able to appreciate their progress. Point out the educational strengths that are developed by completing an in-depth research project. Try, as much as you can, to remove the focus from "winning a contest" to "learning as the true reward."

Example of Student Individual Contract for Extracurricular Project

The undersigned student wishes to complete a documentary project and will meet all expectations as follows:

- Student will read the handbook, worksheets, and learning handouts or packets.
- Student will spend extracurricular hours completing independent research and taking notes, making copies, and completing product. It is understood that student will complete all aspects of the entry on his or her own without assistance from other students or parents.
- Student will attend skills-training sessions and meetings with teacher as scheduled.
- Student will meet target dates for steps of the process. If target dates and/or target date extensions are not met, teacher may ask student to drop participation. Student will coordinate with and inform teacher of any problems that prevent the meeting of target dates and ask for extensions if necessary.

Type of Product: _____ Title of Topic: _____

I agree to the above expectations.

Student: _____

I will support the above student as he/she completes a documentary project.

Teacher: _____ Date: _____

Example of Student Group Contract for Extracurricular Project

The undersigned students wish to complete a documentary project and will meet all group expectations as follows:

- The handbook, worksheets, and learning handouts or packets will be read by the student(s).
- All students will spend extracurricular hours completing independent research, taking notes, making copies, and completing product.
- All students will attend skills-training sessions and other meetings as scheduled with teacher.
- All students will meet target dates for steps of the process. If target dates and/or target date extensions are not met, teacher may ask students to drop participation. Students will coordinate with and inform teacher of any problems that prevent the meeting of target dates.
- Each student understands that his or her commitment to complete the research and product is not only to the teacher, but also to every other member of the group.
- Work will be divided fairly among all members of the group, and each student will do his or her fair share for the project.
- The group will meet regularly and often and take advantage of all available forms of communication (phone, e-mail). All members will attend group meetings and participate fully.
- Each member of the group will be respectful of every other member of the group at all times.
- No money will be spent unless all members are consulted. If a contest is entered and won, all prize money will be split equally among participants.

Type of Product: _____ Title of Topic: _____

I agree to the above expectations.

Student 1: _____ Student 2: _____

Student 3: _____ Student 4: _____

Student 5: _____

I will support the above students as they complete a documentary project.

Teacher: _____ Date: _____

Timeline for Student Documentary

Target Expectation	Target Date	Teacher Initial Minimum Complete
Steps 1 and 2 (1 Week): ■ Read handbook and complete worksheets. ■ Choose Topic. ■ Create File System. ■ Copy bibliography forms.		
Step 3: (2 Weeks) ■ Read handbook and complete keyword brainstorm. ■ Do background research with minimum of at least one encyclopedia/general reference work and two secondary sources. ■ Take notes on research, emphasizing timeline of events. ■ Use bibliography forms for each source. ■ Focus topic.		
Step 4: (2–4 Weeks) ■ Read handbook and complete research leads worksheet. ■ Collect at least a dozen (preferably more) primary sources, analyze and take notes, filling in bibliography forms as you go.		

Target Expectation	Target Date	Teacher Initial Minimum Complete
▪ Begin collecting and scanning/digitizing graphics. Note saved name on back of each. File hard copy in graphics file. Make sure source is noted.		
Step 5: (2 Weeks) ▪ Read handbook. ▪ Search the Internet for primary sources, graphics, and information.		
Step 6: (1 Week) ▪ Read handbook. ▪ Write a minimum of two letters requesting information and/or interviews.		
Step 7: (1–2 Weeks) ▪ Read handbook. ▪ Search available databases. ▪ Search for minimum of two periodical articles, print, or copy and file. Take notes/highlight. ▪ Fill in bibliography forms as you go.		

Target Expectation	Target Date	Teacher Initial Minimum Complete
Step 8: (1 Week) ■ Read handbook. ■ Make copies of video log and fill in for footage clips. ■ Search for professionally produced documentaries, other videotape, laser disc, or CD-ROM video footage. ■ Fill out bibliography forms.		
Step 9: (2 Weeks) ■ Read handbook ■ Conduct at least one videotaped interview of a primary or secondary source. ■ Fill out bibliography sheet for interview(s). ■ Begin filming any graphics (stills) that require camera movement for emphasis (zoom, pan, etc.) or any other graphics that could not be scanned or digitized (Note: If not digitally editing, film all graphics *in order* of storyboard; see Step 11).		
Step 10: (1–3 Weeks) ■ Read handbook. ■ Write the script.		

Target Expectation	Target Date	Teacher Initial Minimum Complete
Step 11: (2–3 Weeks) - Read handbook. - Storyboard script and visuals, matching visual shots with words, sounds, and music.		
Step 12: (2–3 Weeks) - Read handbook. - Learn the basics of operating a camcorder. - Film visuals. - Film on location, if possible.		
Step 13: (2–3 Weeks) - Import stills, capture video. - Record narration. - Edit, mixing sound and visual images with titles and special effects. - Print to VHS tape.		
Step 14: (1 Week) - Write bibliography and process paper. - Complete student self-assessment.		

Educational Multimedia and Copyright Law

Under United States copyright legislation (the Copyright Act of 1976), exclusive rights are given to copyright owners. The law has permitted, however, a "fair use" exemption in order to protect free speech and promote scholarly research and learning. The U.S. House of Representatives' Subcommittee on Courts and Intellectual Property, Committee on the Judiciary, adopted a nonlegislative report in 1996 that related to fair use guidelines for educational multimedia.

Under fair use guidelines, teachers and students may use portions of copyrighted works for their multimedia projects without seeking authorization from the copyright holder. Factors used to consider whether a use is a "fair use" include consideration of the purpose and intent of the use—such use must be strictly of a nonprofit educational nature. Secondly, the amount of the original work being used must be held to guidelines:

- **Motion media** (Professionally produced or distributed videotape, CD-ROM, etc.): Use must be less than 10% or three minutes of the copyrighted work, whichever is less.
- **Text:** Use must be less than 10% or 1,000 words, whichever is less.
- **Music, Lyrics, and Music Video:** Use must be less than 10%, but in no event more than 30 seconds, or the music and lyrics from an individual musical work.
- **Illustrations and Photographs:** Use must be no more than five images by an individual artist or photographer. When using photos and illustrations from a published collective work, not more than 10% or 15 images, whichever is less, may be reproduced.

Educators and students using portions of copyrighted works in multimedia productions *must* include on the opening screen of their program and in any accompanying material (bibliography) the following notice:

Materials in this presentation have been included under the fair use exemption of the U.S. Copyright Law and have been prepared according to the multimedia fair use guidelines and are restricted from further use.

Educators and students must credit sources within the multimedia presentation itself, as well as in the accompanying bibliography, although such notice within the work may be combined and shown in the credits section. Although this has not been spelled out in the fair use guidelines, when using excerpts from professionally produced documentaries or video, it is good practice to credit such work with a title in the lower right-hand or left-hand corner while such footage is on-screen. This also assists the viewer (or judge) in determining what is student-produced footage and what has been used from other sources.

The portion of the guidelines most bothersome for student- or teacher-produced documentaries is the music policy. If using background music throughout a multimedia presentation, it will very often go over the 30-second fair use guideline. For this reason, it is recommended that students and educators either use music that is already in the public domain or obtain permission from the copyright owner.

Only a limited number of copies, including the original, may be made under the fair use guidelines. For all uses, there may be no more than two use copies and one additional preservation copy. In addition, one copy may be made for each principal creator of the presentation (school, teacher, and each student). Multimedia presentations cannot be commercially distributed or reproduced unless written authorization has been obtained from copyright holder(s). Also, they may not be used over electronic networks, except for:

- remote instruction to students enrolled in curriculum-based courses; and
- over an educational institution's secure electronic network, provided such network is secure and technologically limited by a password or PIN.

These guidelines do not apply to works in the public domain. Public domain works include those produced by the U.S. government or those on which the copyright has expired.

For further explanation and the full set of guidelines, visit http://www.libraries.psu.edu/mtss/fairuse/guidelinedoc.html.

Technology Support

First, assess the technology that your school can provide for this project. If you do not have access to the necessary computer hardware and software for editing, you will have to make arrangements for students to do linear editing in-camera, assemble editing, or have them create a computerized or photographic slideshow for their documentary.

Another option is to use an edit controller. If only one computer station with editing hardware and software is available, you will not be able to have every group engage in digital editing because the lack of access will create time constraints. Consider telling students that the project with the best research will be chosen to create a digitally edited movie. Remaining groups would use one or more of the above suggestions for linear editing or slideshows.

In addition, it is recommended that, before introducing digital editing to students, the teacher create (and print to VHS) a mini-project using the technology.

Terminology

Accelerator: A graphics accelerator is a piece of hardware within your computer that speeds up the processing and display of graphics.

Analog: Television broadcasting, VCRs, camcorders, and phone transmission have conventionally used analog technology to transmit signals. Analog signals use current or voltage that is continually fluctuating, with an infinite number of values between given video levels. Modems change the analog transmission of the phone line into digital information that can be read by the computer, and vice-versa. To edit video that has been recorded on a standard VHS tape, the computer's video card must be able to "capture" analog transmission and digitize it. To print to standard analog VCR or camcorder using VHS tape, the computer's video card must change the digital information back to analog to be transmitted to the external device.

Antialiasing: This process is used to average out pixels, providing a smooth transition between images.

Assemble Editing: Linear editing that is accomplished by using a source VCR and a record VCR, and manually playing back and recording from one machine to the other.

Audio Video Interleaving (AVI): In digital video editing, audio, and video data for each frame must be placed together for smooth playback. This is the file format for digital video and audio under Microsoft Windows. Movies created on the desktop are commonly saved as .AVI files.

Bit: The basic unit of digital data.

Bitmap: A graphic image made up on individual color or monochrome pixels. These images are created with rows and columns that form a matrix of pixels, or dots.

Capture: The process of bringing video or audio signals into a computer and converting them to digital format.

CD-ROM: This is digital data that has been stored on a CD. It has Read-Only Memory, so data that is encoded on the CD cannot be changed. Each CD-ROM holds up to 680 megabytes of data.

Clip: A section of a captured video.

CODEC: This video compression driver compresses a video file for storage and then decompresses it for playback. This process saves storage space on the computer.

Color Keying: To create special effects, one scene is superimposed over another. An example of this is when a weatherman is filmed in front of a blue background. During editing, the blue is taken out and the weatherman is superimposed over a shot of a map or other graphic.

Composite Video: A color video signal that transmits all color information. Typical television systems are NTSC, PAL, and SECAM.

Compression: A process of storing data in the computer by reducing the number of bits in the data.

Contrast: Refers to the range between lightest tones and darkest tones in an image. Can be used to bring out or soften elements (such as print words or flaws in photo).

Device Driver: This is software that is loaded onto the computer when installing a peripheral device such as a printer or scanner. It enables the computer to recognize and communicate with the device.

Digital: Signals that are represented by a set of distinct numerical values, as opposed to a continuously fluctuating current or voltage (analog).

Digital Video (DV): Transmits signals by the use of computer-readable binary numbers.

Encoding: The process of creating a compressed file.

Edit Controller: A device that is used for editing between a source VCR and a record VCR. By controlling the recording process so that scenes are played in a preset order, it can create a new, edited tape. The advantage this device gives is one of greater precision in starting and stopping, eliminating snow and jumps that sometimes appear when doing assemble editing.

Firewire: Firewire, or I.Link, are brand names for IEEE P1394, a serial connection to your computer that allows a high-speed rate of data transfer that can accommodate streaming data from digital devices (not analog devices). Information from digital cameras, video discs, camcorders, and other sources can be downloaded directly into the computer through the IEEE P1394.

Flying-Erase Heads: This is one of the most important features on a videocassette recorder (VCR). They allow for clean transitions between scenes and minimize image disturbances, like snow, between clips.

Frame: A single, complete picture in video or film.

Frequency: The rate at which information is transmitted. Normally expressed in cycles per seconds, or Hertz (Hz).

Full-Motion Video: Video that is played at 30 frames per second (NTSC signal) or 25 frames per second (PAL signal).

Generation Loss: Linear editing enables the production of one print at a time, copying a master tape and saving to another tape. Generation refers to the number of copies between a copy and its master. When a copy is made of a copy, it loses sharpness and resolution. Each generation farther away from the master tape has a poorer quality. A copy made in linear editing is already a second-generation tape.

GIF: A file format for saving graphic images, known for its compression and ability to save and display multiple images. The GIF is not the best format to use for photographs and documents because it is limited in the number of distinct colors (256, with some additional available through the color palette) that can be used. GIF is often used for saving text-based images, clip art, or animation because these graphics do not require millions of colors.

In-Camera Editing: A process of shooting scenes in the order of the storyboard. It requires carefully positioning the tape at the end of the previous scene, a difficult and time-consuming process. If voice-over is needed, it must be audio-dubbed when shooting is finished or spoken during filming.

Interpolated Resolution: The process of adding pixels to an image to improve resolution in order to add detail and sharpness to the image.

JPEG: This abbreviation stands for Joint Photographic Expert Group. Provides high-quality compression of pictures. One of the preferred forms of storage for scanned photos.

Linear Editing: The editing of video by playing scenes back one at a time and recording as they are playing. Can be accomplished manually (in-camera or assemble editing), or can be done using a device called an edit controller.

Lossy Compression: During certain types of compression, some of the data in the video is discarded in order to minimize storage space. When the data is decompressed, it is considered lossy when the result is not the same quality as the original data.

MPEG: This abbreviation stands for Motion Picture Expert Group. Provides compression on a frame-to-frame basic, yielding VCR-quality video. MPEG2 is a higher standard, yielding broadcast-quality video. For purposes of playback on a VCR/TV, MPEG is suitable and takes less computer space.

Nonlinear Editing: This is a method of editing that uses a computer to change the order or length of clips; add sound, transitions, and titling; and create a finished linear movie. It is called nonlinear, meaning "random," because the storyboard of shots can be rearranged over and over again.

NTSC: The standard of commercial color television broadcasting in the United States. The format has 525 scan lines, a 60-Hz frequency, frame frequency of 1/30 of a second. The broadcast bandwidth is 4 MHz. The resolution of NTSC broadcasting is 320 x 525.

PAL: Standing for Phase-Alternating Line, this is the video broadcasting format used in most of Western Europe, Australia, and other countries. Offers 625 lines of resolution at 25 frames per second. It is incompatible with NTSC.

Pixel: A single point of an image, having a single color value. The minimum element of a digital graphic.

Pixelation: The point at which graphics are enlarged too much. Individual pixels are obvious and blurring and "boxing" may occur.

Plug-ins: Software programs that give additional new features and effects to software programs. They attach to the existing software and operate as if they are a part of it.

Radius: In referring to digital photography, radius is the number of pixels that are sharpened by a graphics filter.

RCA Connector: Cables that connect the output jacks of audio/visual equipment (like VCRs or camcorders) to the input jacks of another device. These cables are color-coded: yellow for video, red and white for audio (both together for stereo).

Real-Time NLE: These editing systems give you effects that do not need to be integrated into the video. You can play video directly from the storyboard out to tape. Most NLE systems require a "producing" or "processing" time before output or playback is possible.

Render: In digital video, the process of linking all effects (audio, titling, etc.) of the video into a format that can be published to VHS tape or other media.

Resolution: Refers to the number of pixels per unit of area. The higher the resolution, the finer the detail in an image.

S-Video: This type of video transmission is an alternative that can be used instead of composite video in Hi8, S-VHS, DVD, and some laser disc formats.

Streaming: The process of transferring digital video data over the Internet that can be viewed on a computer or a monitor.

Threshold: The difference in brightness between two pixels before they are sharpened by a graphics filter. If threshold is "0," all pixels in the image are sharpened. The higher the threshold, the more blending of contrast areas.

TIFF: Standing for Tagged Image File Format, this is another form of storage for color or black and white images. It is not as commonly used as JPEG, and sometimes is not accepted by software programs.

TWAIN: A widely used program that allows for scanning of images into software programs like Adobe Photoshop.

Video Capture Card: Computer hardware that lets you record video and save it to your computer's hard drive.

Voice-Over: The process of adding sound to a scene and using it instead of, or in addition to, the sound that was originally recorded.

White Balance: A method to help camcorders adjust video for accurate color in different lighting circumstances. This should be performed before any recording by holding a piece of white paper up to the lens of the camcorder.

Recommendations for Nonlinear Editing Systems

If you're investing in a new computer system, ask for one packaged with a video capture card that has in *and* out analog capability. The graphics card should have at least 4 megabytes and support Direct Draw Overlay. You may also want to invest in an IEEE P1394 port (sometimes known as a firewire), but if you don't use a digital camcorder you will probably not need this connection in the immediate future. Get a minimum Pentium II (*stay away from Celeron*) with at least a 266-Mhz speed. Athlon processors (slower, but also less expensive) will work with the right capture card, but check on compatibility beforehand. The best bet for a system that would not need updating in the near future would be a Pentium III with 733 Mhz or higher speed. A minimum of 128 megs of RAM is required, with at least a 10-gigabyte hard drive. You will also need a sound card that allows for audio recording and speakers. You will certainly want a CD-ROM drive, and may want to invest in a CD-RW drive, which allows you to save to a CD.

Upgrading Existing Systems

The best advice I can offer for upgrading a system is "Look before you leap." Compatibility problems are very common, especially with computers that have integrated graphics on the motherboard. To minimize or solve conflicts, check specifications on the product and make sure you have downloaded the latest drivers from your system's vendor.

Video Capture Cards

Video capture hardware can be internally installed on the motherboard or come as an external peripheral device. The hardware can handle analog input/output, digital input/output, or a combination of both. They range in price from just under $100 to over $5,000.

Internal or External?
There are some advantages to purchasing an external capture device. It could be moved from one computer to another (providing you download the drivers and software on each). It is easier to access, although some

internal cards are now coming with an external "breakout box," a device that connects to the back of the graphics card with a thick cable and gives you easier access for connecting RCA cables. Portability may, however, be a drawback because the device could tend to "walk away" in a high-traffic or unsupervised area.

Digital, Analog, or Both?

DV is going to give you the highest quality capture and output, but keep in mind that historical footage is often found in VHS format. Until the digital revolution is over and VHS is a thing of the past, you will need to be able to import analog footage. There are some new graphics cards that accept both, but keep in mind that DV editing requires more storage space on the hard drive.

MPEG1, MPEG2, M-JPEG?

For printing to VHS tape, you will want the capability to compress to an MPEG1 codec. This will take less hard drive space than an MPEG2, which is a superior, broadcast-quality compression. The quality of an MPEG1 product is just as suitable for showing on a standard television/VCR. M-JPEG needs at least 2–3 gigabytes of space for a half-hour video. In addition, it has "lossy" compression, meaning it drops frames to minimize its size. In contrast, the MPEG1 format only requires 300–600 megabytes of space for the same amount of video.

Video graphics cards often come packaged with editing software. The combination packages are a good buy for the beginner. You will not only spend less on the combination than if you bought each separately, but the manufacturers have also (hopefully) eliminated any conflicts between the graphics card and the editing software. Some analog graphics capture cards that have been reviewed by magazines such as *Videomaker* and *PCWorld* include:

Pinnacle's Studio DC10+ (http://www.pinnaclesys.com). This is an internal capture card with input and output for analog video as well as S-Video. Cost is about $150. It uses an M-JPEG codec and needs about 2–7 gigabytes of hard drive space for a half-hour of video. Maximum resolution is 640 x 480. This comes packaged with Pinnacle's Studio software. Pinnacle has long been one of the top names in professional video editing. The *PCWorld* reviewer noted some problems with dropped frames, causing the video to look jumpy at times. Decreasing the resolution and using a high-speed processor helps.

Matrox Marvel G400-TV (http://www.matrox.com/mga). At about $300, this is an internal card that saves to M-JPEG format. Resolution is high at 720 x 480 and requires 2–3.5 GB for a half-hour of video. It comes packaged with Avid Cinema, an easy-to-use editing software that has been on the market for a number of years. *PCWorld* noted minor problems with dropped frames, probably because of the M-JPEG codec; but, in spite of this, they recommended the graphics card because it accelerates 2–D and 3–D graphics performance and includes a breakout box.

Pinnacle's DV500 (http://www.pinnaclesys.com). This one is a bit pricey at $1,000, but it seldom drops frames and gives high-quality output. This card also provides IEEE P1394 ports for downloading digital video and a breakout box with analog inputs (output must be to a digital device). It comes packaged with Adobe's Premier RT 5.1 editing software, a very difficult program for the beginner to learn. The Pinnacle card offers a "preview" mode for digital capture that stores a low-resolution version of clips for editing. After editing is completed, the card will capture the full-resolution video, make edit changes, and output finished product.

Dazzle's DVC (http://www.dazzle.com). At $250, this comes packaged with Ulead's VideoStudio. This is an external device that saves in M-PEG1 format at a resolution of 352 x 240. It needs 300–600 MB of hard drive space for 30 minutes of video. VideoStudio was difficult to learn without a manual, so I used MGI's VideoWave III software instead, but had some minor glitches (pixelation) during output to tape. Once tricky transition effects were eliminated from the video, however, it worked great and output quality was excellent. Dazzle has informed me that they are working on their own editing program to package with the hardware.

Editing Programs

Stand-alone editing programs are relatively inexpensive, but come without the capture card. The downside is that there is a potential for conflicts between the program and capture hardware. For this reason, it is recommended that requirements and suggestions for capture hardware be investigated before the purchase of a stand-alone program. I liked using MGI's VideoWaveIII and the newer VideoWaveIV. Priced at about $100, the software offers a multitude of special effects, such as the ability to layer video clips and vary their transparency, or to remove a solid-colored background from the clip and replace it with a different background (called chroma or color keying). The downside is that the program does not include a timeline. Timelines show all the different elements of the work in progress (titles, sound, etc.) in a graphic form, making it easier to manipulate them. VideoWave uses a storyboard format, which makes it easy to switch the order of scenes, but more cumbersome to make small edits in matching the length of clips to audio, background music, and so forth. The program also allows the user to extract a still shot from a video clip and save it as a JPEG graphic, a nice technique for introducing speakers. (*One important note:* Make sure that your editing program allows you to add still images to your storyline so that students can import JPEG images they have scanned or saved from the Internet.)

Demos and Free Plug-ins

If you're interested in trying out a few editing programs by downloading demos from the Internet or in seeing Quicktime movies about the applications, go to http://www.videoguys.com/free.shtml. This site (last checked in February 2001) features links to free demos for Adobe's Premiere 5.1, ADS MediaStudio 6.0, and Vegas Video. The site also has comparisons of hardware/software, price list, and catalog for purchasing.

Step 1

Introduction to Elements of a Good Documentary and Choosing a Topic

So, You Want to Make a Documentary!

A *documentary* is a work of film that deals with real life, not fiction. There are no actors. A documentary can be about a historical topic like the Civil War, or it can be about a present-day situation, event, or condition, such as prison overcrowding. Good documentaries have many elements in common:

- Stills (photographs) that have been put into the documentary as scanned or digitized nonmoving images. These are usually primary source photographs that relate directly to the subject of the documentary.
- Stills (photographs) that have been filmed and have camera movement that emphasizes certain features of the photograph(s). See section on camera techniques.
- A variety of types of shots (close-up, medium, wide, etc.) and camera movement that serve to make the documentary visually pleasing.
- On-location shots that either serve as background for an on-screen narrator (for example, during the introduction or conclusion) or relate to the script.
- Video footage, usually primary source, that is related to the topic or event.

1

- Sound bytes from experts or people who have first-hand accounts or can explain something about the topic or event. These interview subjects are called "talking heads" because they are seen on-screen from the shoulders up.
- Background music that is related in some way to either the subject or the mood of the documentary. The music should add emphasis to the narration.
- Sound effects that emphasize the script or narration.
- Titles that either identify talking heads, credit sources of video footage, or present basic information that adds to the viewer's understanding.
- Introduction and conclusion that make the point of the documentary clear to the viewer.
- Narrated script that gives the viewer information about the topic.
- Narrated or titled transitions that help ease the viewer from one subtopic to another.
- Title screen that gives the title of the documentary and names the producers and filmmakers.
- Credits screen (usually rolling) that identifies the sources of photographs, video footage, music, sound effects, and also gives credit to talking heads and others who are on-screen or have been influential in the development of the documentary.

Elements of a Documentary Worksheet

In order to create a good documentary, you must fully understand what a good documentary looks like. There is no better way to do this than to watch one, paying attention to the various elements that are blended to create interest and get the message of the documentary across to viewers. To complete the worksheet on the opposite page, obtain a videotaped copy of a good documentary. (Ken Burns is one of the best producers of documentaries in the business, and his series on the history of baseball as well as the Civil War are easily obtained in most video outlets or school videotape libraries.) Watch a segment of a documentary video (at least 10–15 minutes) and make notes on the elements that you observe using the Elements of a Documentary worksheet.

Elements of a Documentary Worksheet

Stills: How has the documentary used photographic images? _____

_____

On still shots, what types of camera movement do you observe? _____

_____

_____

What type of shots (wide, medium, close-up) do you observe? _____

_____

Moving Footage: What type of moving footage does the documentary contain?

_____

Music: What do you notice about the music? Is it constant, or are there pauses?

_____

Sound Effects: What sound effects do you notice, and how are they used?

_____

Titles: How are titles used in the documentary? _____

_____

Narration: How does the narration provide transitions from one scene to another?

_____

What kind of information is presented in the narration? _____

_____

Interview(s): How are interviews used in the documentary? _____

_____

Camera Shots

A good documentary will include several different types of camera shots. Varying the shots serves two purposes. First, using various types of camera shots makes the film visually pleasing to the viewer and helps to promote interest in the topic. Second, the camera can be used to emphasize, or highlight, specific aspects of the photograph or graphic being filmed. For example, a shot might begin from a wide view of a battlefield to show the geography or extent of battle, then move in to a medium view to show a specific soldier, and finally might move in to a close view of the soldier's hand tightly gripping a rifle. The three shots in sequence would bring the viewer into the film subject and create an emotional impact.

Types of Shots

- **Wide Shot:** Usually used on location for showing scenery or geography or to establish the beginning of a location shoot (letting the viewer know where the action is taking place).
- **Medium Shot:** Shows person or subject, plus a bit of surroundings.
- **Close Shot:** Used for interviews (shows a bit of shoulders plus head) or for stills. Use very close, tight shot (head or feature of photo) for emphasis.
- **Macro Close-Shot:** Very, very close—shows extreme detail. Used for exaggerating details on stills.
- **Zoom:** Camera movement that moves in closer or out to a wider view.
- **Pan:** Camera movement that moves horizontally side to side.
- **Tilt:** Camera movement that moves vertically up and down.
- **Cut-Ins:** A brief close-up of a person or object that is a part of the action of the wider shot. An example would be going from a medium view of two people who are seated at a table to a cut-in of a macro close shot showing one person's fingers nervously drumming on the tabletop.
- **Cutaways:** A shot taken of a person or object that is apart from the main action of the wider shot, but related to it. An example would be showing a close shot of an interview subject talking about participating in a protest of the Vietnam War, then switching to a cutaway shot of primary source footage of an actual protest scene.

Photo courtesy of the National Archive

This World War II **wide shot** shows the U.S.S. Franklin being attacked by Japanese kamikaze pilots on March 19, 1945.

A **medium shot** of the same scene puts more emphasis on the soldiers as they helplessly watch.

A **close-up shot** eliminates the background and focuses completely on the soldiers.

Getting an Idea for a Topic

Selecting a topic for a documentary is a crucial step. To start, brainstorm possible ideas that are appealing or interesting to you. Worksheets in this area of the handbook may be helpful. The idea for a topic must come from your interests because you will be working with the topic for many months, delving into it in greater depth than you have ever done with a project before. If you are competing in National History Day, the topic must also fit the year's history day theme.

The wonderful thing about studying history is that everything on earth (and beyond into space travel) has a history. It is usually easy for students to find an area that interests them and then begin to ask questions about the history connected to it. For example, if you enjoy playing baseball, you might wonder how the game began, what impact Babe Ruth had on the game, or how leagues and professional teams got started. There are many research questions that could be formed from a specific topic coming from the general interest, baseball. Do you love reading science fiction? How about a topic on how historic science fiction ideas later became reality? You get the idea . . . any interest can be tied into history.

Although interest level is a consideration, it is equally important that a topic be researchable. That is, are there primary and secondary sources dealing with the topic that can be easily located? For this reason, it might not be a good idea to choose a topic, say, on a medieval subject. For one thing, you will not find records on medieval events in any local archives. Visual images (vital to a documentary) will be scarce and limited to drawings because there was no photography or video in that era. Your teacher, and a quick Internet search, can be helpful to you in assessing how easy it will be to find primary sources on your topic (see Worksheet on Primary/Secondary Sources).

Lastly, you may want to consider how the topic fits to your own original creativity and thinking and how it ties into current issues. A topic should be easily researchable and have lots of primary sources available, but it should also leave room for an original approach or analysis. Sometimes, underlying issues that tie into a historical topic are still of concern today, as in the case of students who researched a 19th-century factory fire and tied it into the existence of current-day sweatshop working conditions. This tie-in gave the students the opportunity to analyze, and it gave the topic added relevance and importance.

After you have brainstormed possible topics, choose several of the most interesting and complete the Topic Ranking Sheet to assess how each idea stands up as a possible topic. Then, take the three topics that scored the highest on your ranking sheet and begin to write some research questions for each one. Finally, choose one of them as your topic. The idea will later become more refined and may change somewhat, but the final documentary should still be related to the general topic area and should not be changed to an entirely different idea. This is so that background reading and research done early in the project will still be relevant and you will not lose precious research time.

Interest Brainstorm: Put a general area that is of high interest to you in the middle and complete a brainstorm web of topic ideas.

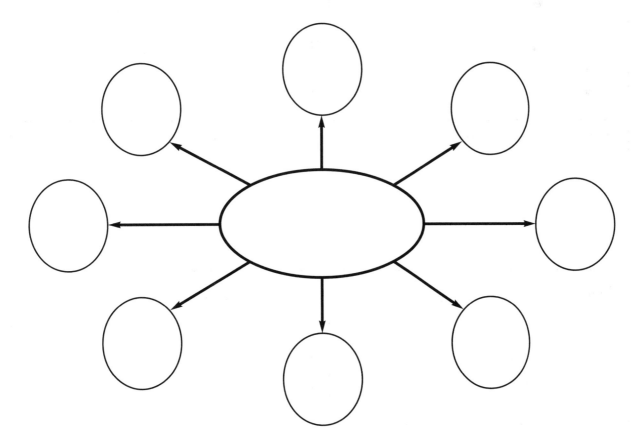

Brainstorm Topic Ideas

See how many historical ideas you can think of:

People	Technology / Science / Inventions
Communication	Exploration / Transportation
Government / Politics / Laws	Wars / Disasters
Problems / Issues / Controversy	Health / Medicine
Culture / Entertainment / Sports	Business / Economics

Topic Ranking Sheet

List your top several interests or brainstorm ideas. Rate them using a 1–5 scale, with 5 being the best fit for the criteria. Add the totals. Which topic will make the best History Day project?

Topic Ideas	Topic is exciting/ interesting to me	Visuals (photos, film) available on topic	Many Primary/ Secondary sources on topic	The topic has ties to a current-day issue/ problem	The topic encourages an original or creative approach	Total Sum for Topic

My chosen topic is:

Because:

Teacher Signature: _____ Date: _____

Step 2

Organize, Organize, Organize!

One of the traits all successful creators of documentaries have in common is their great sense of organization and attention to detail. This section will assist you in keeping track of and using the tons of information you will accumulate. You will also learn to record your sources as you do your research so that you don't go crazy searching for references when you try to compile your bibliography.

The first thing you must do is understand the different housekeeping tasks that are involved in the research process. If you are working individually, you have to take care of all of these tasks as you proceed with research. In a group, while everyone is responsible for accomplishing research, members can divide recordkeeping tasks according to suggested group roles during research. In this way, each member of the group is responsible for specific research and filing duties. All members must coordinate their efforts, however, with others in the group.

Next, establish the file system. Accordion files and plastic tow-as-you-go fileboxes work well, but so does a cardboard box if it is just large enough for manila file folders to stand up in it. Each member of a group involved in a documentary project should have his or her own pocket folder where information is kept until it can be filed in the appropriate folder in the group file system. A specific responsibility for keeping part of the research files up-to-date is assigned to each member of the group.

11

The file system should have the following divisions, each in its own manila folder:

1. Rules/Worksheets/Handouts

This will be where you keep your how-to-do-it packets and information sheets and a copy of the rules for any competition you might be entering.

2. Background Research

This is where you will keep your first notes and basic background information on the general topic. Background research should answer the who, what, when, where, and how of the topic and give a preliminary timeline of events, as well as information on the conditions in society in the era of the topic.

3. Research Leads

This is where you keep notes on resources to hunt for, individuals to track down; libraries with information, and so forth, along with a list of where you have sent for information and copies of letters/e-mails you have sent.

4. Subtopic Research Sections

The number and title of these files will be different for each topic. For example, students researching the Love Canal toxic dump would have folders on: Geography of Area; Timeline of Events; Chemicals; New York State Government Agencies; EPA/Superfund; Community Organizations; Lois Gibbs; Diseases/Health Problems Caused by Contamination; and so on. Within each subsection, you will file notes or copies of important information and documents. Use highlighters to pick out possible captions, quotes, or facts; if the document contains a graphic that you might want to use as a visual image, make an extra copy for your graphics file before highlighting.

5. Graphics File

The graphics file will include a copy of any item that you feel would make a good visual graphic for your documentary. The items could be a printed photo from the Internet, a printed copy of a graphic that you scanned, a photocopy from a book or document, and so forth. This file will certainly include photographs, maps, deeds, letters, and headlines of news articles can also make good visuals for a documentary. On the back of each graphic, you must note important information about the graphic—identify the date the photo was taken, the name of photographer (if known), location, and names of people in the photo. If the graphic has been scanned or saved on disc from the Internet, note the file name under which it was saved. Lastly, in a circle, indicate the bibliography number you assigned to the source. Taking the time to do this now will save you frustration and lost work time later on.

6. Bibliography

This is the most important section to keep up to date. There are a number of forms in this handbook that will help you keep track of your sources as you research. See the page on how-to-do an annotated bibliography, and learn from the start what information you need to record each time you use a source.

You can see from the following bibliography reference forms that there is a slightly different format for specific types of sources you might use in your research. Master copies include forms for books, magazine/newspapers, documents/brochures/pamphlets, interviews, audio-visual or computerized media, letters, and Internet sources. On each form, though, is a circle in which you will put your reference number. Assign *each source* a unique number of your own choosing and write this number in the circle on the form. Also include the circled number on any notes or copies you make of information from this source or on the back of any graphics you take from the source (see "Taking Notes" in Step 3). The information on each form has been arranged in proper order for your bibliography, including any required punctuation.

Master Copies of Bibliography Reference Forms

The following pages contain the master copies of the seven bibliography reference forms: (1) Book Reference Form; (2) Magazine/Newspaper Form; (3) Document, Brochure, or Pamphlet Form; (4) Interview Reference Form; (5) Audio-Visual Reference Form; (6) Internet Reference Form; and (7) Letter or E-Mail Reference Form. **Do not write on these forms!** Copy them as you need them and file in your file system.

Book Reference Form

(Author/Editor, Last Name First) _____ .

(Full Title—Underline) _____ .

(Place of Publication) _____ :

(Name of Publisher) _____ ,

(Year of Publication) _____. **Your Reference Number:**

(Annotation) _____

_____

_____

_____

- -

(Author/Editor, Last Name First) _____ .

(Full Title—Underline) _____ .

(Place of Publication) _____ :

(Name of Publisher) _____ ,

(Year of Publication) _____. **Your Reference Number:**

(Annotation) _____

_____

_____

_____

Magazine/Newspaper Reference Form

(Author/Reporter, Last Name First) _____.

(Title of Article in quotes) "_____"

(Title of Publication—Underline) _____ (no punctuation)

(Date of
Publication)_____
        Day   Month   Year

Volume or
Section: Page No. _____
        Section: Page

Your Reference Number:

Annotation: _____

_____

_____

- -

(Author/Reporter, Last Name First) _____.

(Title of Article in quotes) "_____"

(Title of Publication—Underline) _____ (no punctuation)

(Date of
Publication)_____
        Day   Month   Year

Volume or
Section: Page No. _____
        Section: Page

Your Reference Number:

Annotation: _____

_____

_____

Document, Brochure, or Pamphlet Reference Form

(Agency or Organization
Creating Document) _____.

(Type of Document) _____.

(Title in quotes) "_____,"

(Date of Document) _____.
                   (If no date, put NPD—No Publication Date).

(Name of File, followed
by Archive/Library Found in) _____.

Your Reference Number: ⬭

(Annotation) _____

_____

_____

- -

(Agency or Organization
Creating Document) _____.

(Type of Document) _____.

(Title in quotes) "_____,"

(Date of Document) _____.
                   (If no date, put NPD—No Publication Date).

(Name of File, followed
by Archive/Library Found in) _____.

Your Reference Number: ⬭

(Annotation) _____

_____

_____

Interview Reference Form

(Person Interviewed, Last Name First) _____.

(Telephone or Personal) Interview.   (Date of Interview) _____.

Day   Month   Year

Your Reference Number: (_____)   Permission to Quote Given? _____

Annotation (Include Person's Title and place of business if important): _____

_____

_____

_____

_____

- -

(Person Interviewed, Last Name First) _____.

(Telephone or Personal) Interview.   (Date of Interview) _____.

Day   Month   Year

Your Reference Number: (_____)   Permission to Quote Given? _____

Annotation (Include Person's Title and place of business if important): _____

_____

_____

_____

_____

Audio-Visual Reference Form

(Director/Composer, Last Name First) _____.

(Title of Song in quotes) " _____,"

(Title of CD or Video—underlined) _____.

(Producer of CD or Video) _____, Year of Production _____.

Your Reference Number: ⬭

Annotation: _____

_____

_____

- -

(Director/Composer, Last Name First) _____.

(Title of Song in quotes) " _____,"

(Title of CD or Video—underlined) _____.

(Producer of CD or Video) _____, Year of Production _____.

Your Reference Number: ⬭

Annotation: _____

_____

_____

Internet Reference Form

(Author of Article or Page, Last Name First) _____.

(Title of Article/Page—in quotes) "_____,"

(If known, organization that created web site) _____.

Online. Internet. (Web address in brackets) [_____

_____].

(Date you pulled info from Internet) _____
                                      Day   Month   Year

Your Reference Number:

Annotation: _____

_____

- -

(Author of Article or Page, Last Name First) _____.

(Title of Article/Page—in quotes) "_____,"

(If known, organization that created web site) _____.

Online. Internet. (Web address in brackets) [_____

_____].

(Date you pulled info from Internet) _____
                                      Day   Month   Year

Your Reference Number:

Annotation: _____

_____

Letter or E-Mail Reference Form

(Person Who Sent Letter, Last Name First) _____ to

(Person Who Received Letter, First and Last Name), _____

(Date of Letter) _____.
                     Date   Month   Year

(If found in archive, name of archive & collection) _____.

Your Reference Number: ⬭

Annotation (Include title and place of business of sender and receiver, if important): _____

_____

_____

_____

- -

(Person Who Sent Letter, Last Name First) _____ to

(Person Who Received Letter, First and Last Name), _____

(Date of Letter) _____.
                     Date   Month   Year

(If found in archive, name of archive & collection) _____.

Your Reference Number: ⬭

Annotation (Include title and place of business of sender and receiver, if important): _____

_____

_____

_____

Group Roles During Research Phase

Archivist

- Responsible for maintaining file system. Coordinates with all group members to receive documents they have located or notes they have taken.
- Responsible for finding, copying, printing, scanning, and saving to network or floppy disc primary source documents.
- Assists other group members with analysis of documents.

Source Specialist

- Keeps the bibliographic file up-to-date.
- Coordinates with all group members to check on research sources the group has used and assign each source a bibliographic number.
- Fills in a bibliographic form for each source that has been used.
- Writes analysis of each source for annotated bibliography.
- Word-processes bibliography using proper bibliographic style.

Media Specialist

- Views and logs videotape(s).
- Searches for and finds photographs for use in documentary.
- Makes photocopy or printed copy of photographs found by all members of the group.
- Coordinates with group members to receive photographs and keeps photograph/graphics file up-to-date.
- Finds and saves video/audio from CD-ROM sources or Internet (coordinates with Internet specialist).
- Coordinates with archivist to assess suitability of primary source documents for use as graphics.
- Finds music that is appropriate to time period or topic.
- Films or photographs graphics as necessary or when camera movement is needed to add strength to documentary.

Head Researcher

- Keeps track of and follows up on research leads.
- Orders interlibrary loan books.
- Writes letters to individuals, museums, and organizations that may have information on the topic.
- Conducts historical surveys, creates graphs and charts.
- Makes appointments and writes questions for interviews. Follows up and makes calls as needed.
- Sends thank-you letters to those who have sent information or given interviews.
- Coordinates all members of the group, making sure everyone is on task.

Research Specialist(s)

- Responsible for Specific research tasks, for example, Internet search or database/periodical search and note taking, photocopying, or printing sources.
- Reports back to group and coordinates with Source Specialist (bibliography), Archivist (documents and notes), Head Researcher (research leads), and Media Specialist (film, music, and photo leads).

How to Do an Annotated Bibliography

An **annotated bibliography** is the best way of recording your sources and is required for many history competitions, including National History Day. This type of bibliography is basically a list of all of the sources that you have used in researching and producing your project. The *annotation* is a short description of the source and what you learned or gained from it, along with an evaluation of the usefulness/credibility of the source. Explain in the annotation why you believe something is a primary source, especially if you have found it within a secondary source. The following questions will help you as you think about writing annotations:

- What type of source is this? Is it specific or general? Does it discuss just one aspect of your topic? Is it a source that is generally used by most people when they research your topic?
- How did you use the source in researching/preparing your project? What quotations or graphics did you get from it? (Be Specific!)
- What understanding did you develop from studying this source? Did it give you information you did not find elsewhere?
- Does the information you learned from this source conflict with or disagree with other things you have read? If so, why do you think this happened and which source do you agree with?
- Is the source biased in any way? Why or why not?

A **bias** is a prejudgment or tendency toward a limited perspective on an idea or issue.

Style of Bibliography

Your bibliography references must be listed and follow the most recent edition of one of the following reference style guides: Kate L. Turabian, *A Manual for Writers of Term Papers, Theses, and Dissertations;* or the style guide of the Modern Language Association of America (MLA). The example bibliography page on the page that follows will give you an idea of the way bibliography references are listed. References must be divided between primary and secondary sources and alphabetized by last name of author/organization.

Example of (Parts of) a Bibliography

Primary Sources

Brown, Mike. "Evacuation of Kids Urged," *Niagara Gazette* 2 Aug 1978. Online. Internet. Ecumenical Task Force Collection. [http://ublib. buffalo.edu/libraries/projects/lovecanal/]. 5 February 1999.
Mike Brown was the reporter who first publicized the existence of chemical contamination in residents' homes and yards. This source was very helpful in giving information about the evacuation of pregnant women and small children.

Format for Internet source

Carey, Hugh L. Letter to President Jimmy Carter. 24 July 1980. cc to Commissioner Flacke found in Health Department files, NY State Archives.
In this letter, Carey wrote about the urgent situation in Love Canal. It gave the Governor's point of view and helped us to understand the position of New York State. It discusses the need for federal financial assistance and is a formal request for aid.

Format for letters

"Containment Area." Photograph. Online. Internet. Ecumenical Task Force Collection. [http://ublib.buffalo.edu/libraries/projects/love-canal/]. 30 November 1998.
We used this picture as our last shot because it showed a danger sign, and we wanted to give the impression that parts of the area are still dangerous today.

Gabalski, Anita. Interview. 1 March 1999.
Ms. Gabalski currently works for the New York State Health Department, but during the Love Canal Crisis, she was a citizen participation specialist for the New York State Department of Environmental Conservation. She cleared up much of our confusion as to the location of the evacuations and "rings". She also confirmed for us information about the children's baseball field being built on top of the canal.

Interview format

New York State Department of Health. *Love Canal: A Special Report to the Government and Legislature.* April 1981.

Government publications format

This report gave us many pictures that we used in our video, including shots of houses, testing of small children, and scientists analyzing information. This source also gave us statistics concerning the number of deaths and illnesses at Love Canal. Dr. Beverly Paigen, however, believed the incident of diseases was much higher than was given in this government report and we believed her assessment was more accurate.

Notice student analysis here

Secondary Sources

"Changed Forever by Love Canal," *People.* 7–14 March 1994, 168.

Magazine format

We got the most recent photo of Lois Gibbs from this source and learned what she is doing today. The article gave us the name and location of the nonprofit organization Gibbs works for and enabled us to contact her for an interview.

Fumento, Michael. "EPA Hides Behind Myths of Love Canal," Online. Internet. [http://www.consumeralert.org/fumento/super.htm]. 10 December 1998.

Notice how these students evaluated the source

This source gives the Hooker Chemical point of view and condemns governmental sources. We did not give much weight to the information, however, because even though the writer claimed to be the author of a book titled *Science Under Siege*, we could not definitely identify the web site to a known organization or association that was reputable.

Bibliography written by Mary Grace Albanese, Lidya Yankovskaya, Amanda Beebe, and Jo Klemczak, Best-of-State Winners, Junior Documentary, National History Day, June 1999.

Step 3

Background Research

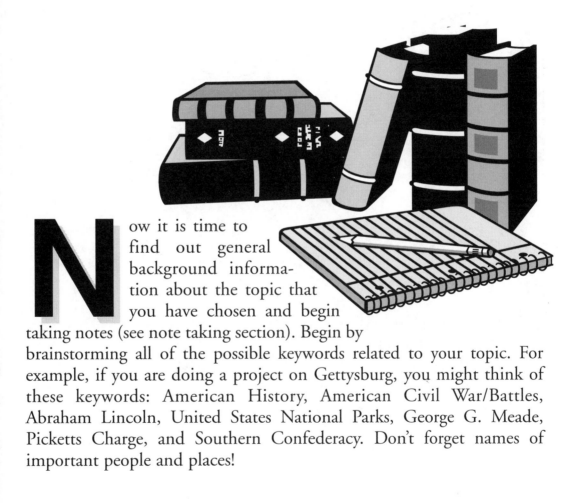

Now it is time to find out general background information about the topic that you have chosen and begin taking notes (see note taking section). Begin by brainstorming all of the possible keywords related to your topic. For example, if you are doing a project on Gettysburg, you might think of these keywords: American History, American Civil War/Battles, Abraham Lincoln, United States National Parks, George G. Meade, Picketts Charge, and Southern Confederacy. Don't forget names of important people and places!

Keyword Brainstorm

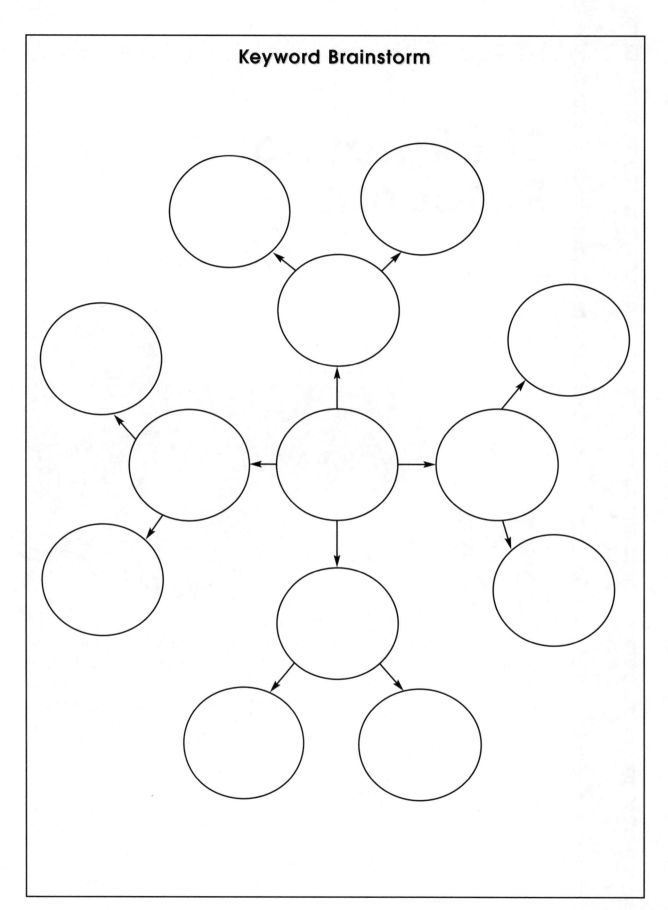

Using your keywords, begin looking up information. You can start with some general reference books like encyclopedias, atlases, or history textbooks. Take notes (see note taking section) and record sources in your bibliography forms, assigning each source its own reference number. You are also going to write the reference number you create for the source in a circle in one of the corners of each page of your notes.

Using an Encyclopedia or General Reference Work

An encyclopedia article will give you an abbreviated overview of the subject. This may assist in giving research leads and a general idea of the topic. Encyclopedia entries should not, however, be used in place of reading more complete books on the topic.

Encyclopedias or general reference works should be thought of as a place where you can find clues and research leads. Cross-referencing terms that are mentioned can help the reader to think of new keywords for searching library catalogues or the Internet. Some encyclopedias may also give a short bibliography of well-known primary and secondary sources on the topic.

The next step is to do a search on a library catalogue. Most libraries, public or school, have computerized catalogues today. These are quite simple to use. The following general rules should apply to most computerized catalogues, but you may want to also check with your librarian.

- **Choose keyword search option.** The reason for this is simple: A keyword search is the most powerful option because it will search all fields of the database.

- **Type in your keyword.** A list of book titles with their respective authors will appear. This list contains only titles that are located in the library. Enter the item number of a title for more information. Keep a list of any titles, with catalogue number, that look like they will be useful. **Watch out for** juvenile fiction or children's books that are not usually accurate or helpful for a research project.

- **If you get too many results from your keyword search, narrow it down by including other keywords.** You can also search by author. It is sometimes helpful to order the list with the most recent publications first.

- **Search other area libraries.** Ask the librarian if their catalogue has an option for searching the catalogues of other area libraries or schools.

- **If you have found books that are available from other libraries**, ask the librarian for the interlibrary loan (ILL) procedures and order them. It usually takes at least two weeks, sometimes longer, to obtain the loan, so don't wait to do this!

- **Repeat this process for all of your keywords.**

- **Retrieve the books from the shelves**. "Eyeball" the book to see if it is something that will be useful for you. Do this by looking at chapter headings, index, and bibliography pages. If the book seems to have good information on your topic, check it out, and take notes or make photocopies of information. Make sure the source is entered in the proper bibliography form and assigned a reference number.

Note Taking

Beginning with the general background stage of research, you should take careful notes and record sources on bibliography forms. General background notes should answer these questions:

- **Who**. What individuals were involved with the topic? What government agencies? What businesses?
- **What**. What happened? What was the timeline of events? What circumstances (cause and effect) led to the event(s)?
- **When**. What year(s) did the event happen? What was going on in the time period? If you picked up news magazines from the time, what would be mentioned? What was the culture of the time period like?
- **Where**. Where did the event(s) happen? Did the geography of the area have an impact, and why?
- **Why**. Why did it happen? Why did it change history? Why was it important?

In addition, you should write down any questions that occur to you as you study the background information and record answers to those questions as you find them. Is there anything that you are learning that is surprising or of great interest to you? Take careful notes about the idea or subtopic and keep it in mind as an area you can focus on during later research.

You should use a new sheet of notepaper for each source you use. Sometimes, if you have found a lot of information, it is also helpful to make a new sheet of notes for each subtopic found within a source so that you can organize the notes better within your research files. Put the number of the source (the number you assigned on your bibliography form) in a big circle at the top right corner on *each page of your notes*. This way, you will always know from what source you took the notes, even if the pages get separated later on.

When you're taking notes, write them as if you were trying to explain something to someone who knows nothing about the subject. Abbreviate whenever you can, but make sure that you will be able to understand the abbreviations later on. If you are copying a direct quote, make sure that you put the words in quotation marks and indicate the page number in the source from which you took the quote.

Some students prefer to copy pages from a book rather than take handwritten notes. It is fine to use this technique if the information you need is extensive, but if you do so you must still take time to read the information and highlight the really important facts or quotations on the photocopy. Students who photocopy everything they can might think they are doing good research, but more pages *does not* equal more learning! To learn, you need to read and analyze the information, not just count the number of pages you have copied.

Plagiarism is when you copy information word-for-word from a source without using quotation marks. In other words, it is trying to make something appear as if it has been written by you; when in reality it was copied directly from another source. It is okay to use quotes; in fact, they are very useful primary sources in a documentary. But, you need to always make sure you know what is a direct quote, cite whose words they are, and keep track of sources in your bibliography.

Background research should include *a minimum* of:

- at least one encyclopedia or general reference work (preferably two); and
- at least two secondary books on your topic.

Focus Your Topic

A focus is really like a camera lens—it's a perspective from which to view material. Focusing a topic brings it into sharp clarity and greater depth. To create a project that is more than just a repetition of material easily found in standard reference books, you need to find a perspective that makes a new understanding of the topic possible. One way to do this is to choose a specific focus on which to concentrate your deeper research. An example of focusing a broader topic would be:

Broad topic: Television programming.
Focus: The impact of television programming on women in the 1950s.

The focus allows you to explore an area of your topic in depth, and it also leads to the development of your own claim or perspective (sometimes called a *thesis*). In the above example, you can see how the focus could easily lead to the student doing some original thinking and analysis about the topic. You can also see how the focus is tied into a current issue—the perception of women that is shown in the media and how that affects them. You could go even further in focusing and explore the way one show (*I Love Lucy*, for example) portrayed or affected women's views of themselves.

The process of developing a focus begins while you are first learning about your topic. As you read and learn about the subject, you should be intentionally looking for possible focal points in the material and writing down these ideas. If a topic is interesting, you can get lost in the research stage and spend large amounts of time reading without getting any closer to a clear focus. To avoid this, when you read or learn about your topic, keep the goal of choosing a focus in your mind and look for possible viewpoints that you can explore in greater depth. Does a focus area tie into current issues? Does it allow for some original thinking to be done, or is it generally well-known knowledge? If you are entering a contest, does the focus area fit in with the contest theme?

Step 4

Collect and Analyze Primary Sources

What is a Primary Source?

A *primary source* is a first-hand account or document directly from the event or time period that is being studied. Examples include a person's diary, the Declaration of Independence, a letter sent from a soldier to his family in time of war, a will, a baptismal certificate, a photograph, a newspaper or magazine article from the time of the event, or a marriage license. Even music or artwork could be considered a primary source if it is from the time period or related to the subject being studied.

You can often find printed books that reprint facsimiles or collections of primary sources. An example would be the many books that have reprinted Eleanor Roosevelt's letters word-for-word or the Civil War diaries that have been published. Sometimes, the topic determines what is or is not a primary source. Eleanor Roosevelt's letters, for example, would be primary sources for research on her life, but they would be secondary sources if your topic was the New Deal (unless they mention or give a perspective on the New Deal specifically).

You can also find primary sources (or copies of them) at archives, libraries, university/college collections, historical societies, town clerk offices, government agencies, museums, and associations or organizations. Many primary source documents have been digitized and placed on the Internet, but you need to be sure the sources on the site are authentic (real documents that have not been altered; see Searching the Internet).

A *secondary source* is an account that was written by someone who has studied the event, but who was not personally involved or present at the time of the event. An example is a history textbook that tells about an event and explains the outcomes and reasons for the event. Primary source documents (hopefully) have been used to create the secondary source, and may even be reprinted in the source. If you use a photograph or a word-for-word quotation from a primary source that is reprinted in a secondary source, you may count it as a primary source. In your bibliography, it would be cited as follows:

"Purchase Tickets Via Erie Railway." Broadside. As found in Divine, Robert A., *America Past and Present*. Glenview, Illinois: Scott, Foresman, 1987.

Broadside: A poster or flyer

Through a collection and study of primary sources, you will construct your own understanding of the person, time, or event and not rely on the understanding of others. In this way, you become a real historian—interpreting events for yourself. Of course, historians also compare their views to those of other historians, but they always refer back to the primary sources whenever possible. This kind of original historical "detective work" is vital to producing a quality documentary.

Documentaries should include visual shots of primary sources. These will most likely be largely photographs and videotape footage, but also may include photos of artwork, headlines, and parts of articles from newspapers, political cartoons, artifacts, letters, tickets, and broadsides. Usually, a primary source "still" will be scanned, photographed with a digital camera, filmed with a camcorder, or saved as a graphic from the Internet. For 20th-century topics, you can find primary source film that may be located on CD-ROMS, laser discs, the Internet, or videotape.

Where to Look for Primary Sources

- State and local archives
- University and college libraries and archives
- Local, county, or state historical societies
- Town, city, or county historians
- Local, state, and federal government offices—for example, the town clerk's office or the federal Environmental Protection Agency
- Museums
- Public libraries
- National archives (http://www.nara.gov)
- Library of Congress (http://memory.loc.gov)
- Presidential libraries
- Internet sites (evaluate the sites carefully)
- Printed in secondary sources
- Collections of postcards or other trivia; scrapbooks in attics
- Veterans groups
- Minutes of community or business organizations
- Local television stations

In-Depth Research

When you have accomplished all the preliminary work, you are ready to begin your in-depth research. The steps in completing your research are simple, and they build on each other much like a set of building blocks stack together to create a tower. By following the suggestions below, you will build a broad base of primary and secondary sources.

First, start with a book that has been written by a historian. The book should have a bibliography, endnotes, or footnotes to indicate the primary sources the author used in his and her research. This will give you a list of many possible sources to investigate in your search, as well as knowledge of what institutions (museums, archives, or universities) have collections of materials relating to your topic. What source did the author use the most? This is probably the most important primary source to obtain. Make a photocopy of the bibliography in the book and use it as your guide to collecting primary sources. Fill out the Research Leads Worksheet.

Next, go to a public or university library. Try to find books the author mentioned. Get staff assistance to request by interlibrary loan if necessary. Microfilmed collections of primary sources are often available through interlibrary loan, as well. Check for addresses of any universities, colleges, archives, or museums that were mentioned in the book's bibliography. If there are, check the organization's web site for digitized collections of sources. Check the *Encyclopedia of Associations* for any organizations that are connected to your topic. Keep track of addresses and leads in the Research Leads section of your file system.

Visit state or local archives or other local history collections. Archives are different than traditional libraries because they contain the original records of an agency or business, or the private papers of an individual. They have usually been donated to the archives so that they can be given proper care and be preserved for future generations. Before visiting archives, you should:

- know what type of records the archive maintains (for example, if it is a state facility, the archive will contain state government documents and papers);
- understand proper procedures for using archival material;
- complete background research so that you will understand the documents you see;
- know what you are looking for; and
- contact the archive ahead of time to ask for assistance in pulling information on your topic from their collections. Sometimes it is best to have an adult make this call for you. During the phone call, ask if there are any finding aids that are available on the topic. Sometimes these aids have been published and are available at public libraries.

Use telephone directories and track down experts on the topic or people who were mentioned by name in bibliographies. You can find secondary experts on historical topics in history departments of most colleges or universities. You can also use a people search on the Internet once you have the names of some of the key players or authors who are involved in the topic. Interview in person if possible, or by phone or e-mail.

Researchers/college professors should always be asked how you can obtain primary sources on your topic. Interviews of people who have first-hand knowledge, however, should wait until you feel you have learned quite a bit about your topic and have some good investigative questions (see interview section).

Research is like detective work—you find clues that lead you to the primary sources so that you can begin to analyze the topic by examining the original sources of information.

General Archival Policies

- Coats, hats, notebooks, purses, and book bags are usually stored in lockers so that documents do not accidentally (or otherwise) leave the facility.
- Patrons usually must sign in and indicate the purpose of the research.
- Food and drinks are not allowed in the research area.
- The use of pens is not allowed, so come prepared with pencil and paper. Sometimes, the archive will want patrons to use writing materials provided by the facility.
- When handling photographs or other very old materials, patrons will be asked to wear white gloves. This is because each time we touch something, our hands leave a trace of oil and acid on the document. We don't see this with our eyes, but over time, residue from hands can fade, yellow, or even disintegrate documents and photos.
- Do not make any marks, erasures, or other changes in the documents.
- Ask for assistance with photocopying and be prepared to pay a fee. Some facilities allow patrons to take digital photos with a personal camera, or even allow them to bring in a laptop computer and scanner.
- Keep records in their present files and arrangement. Ask how the archives would like you to indicate records you would like photocopied. Sometimes they will have acid-free "bookmarks" available.
- Keep materials flat on the table, and handle with extreme care.

Example of How a Book With A Bibliography Can Lead to Primary Sources and Research Leads

Anderson, Mary, as told to Mary N. Winslow. *Women at Work*. Minneapolis, University of Minnesota Press, 1951. Reprint. Westport, CT: Greenwood Press, 1973.

> Gives names of important secondary sources.

Cobb, Ellen Clay to Levi F. Waldron. Letters 1867–90. Historical Society of Whitehall Collection, Isaac C. Griswold Public Library, Whitehall, NY.

> Gives information on where you can find collections of primary sources.

Interviews, circa 1970. Oswego County Oral History Interview Collection, Penfield Library, SUCO Special Collections, State University of NY at Oswego.

Jones, Mary Harris. *Autobiography of Mother Jones*. Reprint. New York: Arno, 1969.

> Autobiographies are primary sources if the person was involved in the topic of research.

National Women's Trade Union League of America. *Proceedings. Biennial Conventions 1909, 1911*. Chicago: National Women's Trade Union League, 1909, 1911.

> Gives name of organization that kept records—important research lead!

U.S. Department of Labor, Women's Bureau. Bulletin No. 66. Beyer, Clara E. *History of Labor Legislation for Women in Three States*. Washington, D.C.: Government Printing Office, 1929.

U.S. Department of Labor, Women's Bureau. *Toward Better Working Conditions For Women, Methods and Policies of the National Women's Trade Union League of America*. Bulletin no. 252. Washington, D.C.: Government Printing Office, 1953.

> Gives the name of a government agency that would be important to contact, as well as the bulletin number for a publication you could ask for when contacting them. This contact might also lead to possible phone interviews. Government agencies are usually willing to send free information to students.

Research Leads Worksheet

1. Museums, organizations, or associations that might have information on my topic:

2. Books (With author, publisher, etc.) on my topic:

3. Primary source collections are located at these colleges, universities, or archives:

4. Government agencies that might have information:

5. Individuals who might have knowledge of my topic:

Analyzing Historical Documents/Sources

When conducting historical research, it is important that the researcher analyze the document or source for accuracy. Sources can be *biased*, meaning that the author had a self-interest, prejudice, or reason for believing the way he or she did when writing the item. This is especially important when working with Internet sources (see p. 23). Historians should analyze each source that is used during research by asking and answering some of the following questions:

- Who wrote the document?
- How was the author involved in the event or topic? Is he or she a first-hand witness? An expert on the topic?
- If the source is a web page, can you get back to a home page to verify the identity of the author? (See section on Internet research.)
- Does the writer have a personal point of view or bias?
- Do you notice an emotional tone in the writing? For example, does the writer seem angry? Is he or she using sarcasm or making insults?
- Why was the document written?
- Did anyone benefit in some way from the writing of the document?
- Is there a political purpose for the creation of the document? A commercial or financial incentive?
- What was the time between the event being studied and the writing of the document?
- Is the meaning of the document clear?
- Is the writing of the document appropriate for your needs?
- Does the information in the document conflict or contradict information from other sources? Can you verify the information in this document by using other sources?

Conflict or contradict: to clash, or be opposite to

Reading Documents from the 18th or Early 19th Century

Primary source documents from earlier centuries will have different handwriting or typefaces than we are used to today. Very often, the letter *s* appears to be an *f* in early documents. This particularly happened when there was a double letter *s*, for example, in the word *assigned*. In ancient documents, the word would look like *afsigns*. The *f* as a letter *s* would also occur at the beginning of words. The word *success* would therefore look like *fuccefs, or fucceff*.

This can be confusing to those who are not used to reading historical documents. Handwritten documents were also very neatly written in cursive handwriting, so even though you may spend time getting used to the *f*, you can still enjoy reading the document. Historians often use magnifying glasses to simplify reading of manuscripts and maps.

A Word on Collecting Photographs or Graphics

It often happens that students who are producing a documentary do not realize they are going to use a particular photo, map, or other graphic until after they have written their script. For this reason, you should have a large collection of graphics (photos, cartoons, maps, scanned/digitized images, etc.) that you have gathered during your research.

When copying and saving graphics, it is extremely important that you caption them so that you will know exactly what the photograph is depicting and where you got it. The easiest way to keep track of your photos is to

The Japanese surrender aboard the U.S.S. Missouri at the end of World War II. Online: http://www.nara.gov/exhall/wwii/surrender/surrender.html

print out or make a copy of the photo and then (in pencil, so the ink does not bleed through) put the following information on the back:

- reference number of the source where you obtained the photo;
- identification of who is in the photo, what is happening in the photo, date and where and when it was taken (if you know), and why it was taken; and
- if you scanned or otherwise saved the photo to a computer file, the file name under which it was saved. Too many times, students save or scan large quantities of graphics, only to find out later that they can't locate the right image because they have no clue what name it was saved under.

Keep your graphics in a separate file folder and take care to store them so that they do not get crumpled or bent. The important thing is to keep them flat and in good condition. There is nothing worse than trying to scan or film a graphic that has been wrinkled, torn, or mutilated.

Directions for Scanning Images

When you find photographs in books or copies of other documents that you might wish to use in your documentary, you should scan them directly from the source whenever possible. Scanning from the source gives you a better quality image and also allows you to grab the image in color without the expense of color copying. You will probably want to begin scanning images early in your research process. Scanners work by digitizing the image and transmitting the data to a photo editing program. There are many such programs on the market, but Adobe Photoshop is one of the most popular and offers many features for editing and refining the image. Programs like Picture Window (made by Digital Light & Color) or Corel's Photo House are also very popular. Programs often come with scanners and are automatically installed when the scanner drivers are installed, so check your computer's hard drive. Most editing programs use procedures similar to those on the following page:

- Open the program.
- Select FILE and then IMPORT (this may also be called ACQUIRE IMAGE).
- In the IMPORT dialogue box, select source from which photo will be obtained. You may see the name of your scanner or you may see something called TWAIN, which is the device that allows your computer to receive images from the scanner. Select and hit OK.
- You will now see a scanning screen. Select PREVIEW option.
- You will now see your image. See if there is a dotted box that you can use to select the portion of the page or image that you want. Drag it and position it as you wish and then click FINAL SCAN. The scanner will make another pass over the image and import only the portion you have selected into your photo editing program.
- If you can select the type of image here, select SHARP B and W. PHOTO or SHARP COLOR PHOTO as your best option.
- X-OUT of Scanning Screen or minimize it if it is not done automatically. If you did not select the exact portion of image you need in the scanning step, you can crop the image now. Select the dotted box on the toolbar. Click and drag the box so that it is around the portion of image that you want. Select IMAGE on the menu bar and scroll down and select CROP. The image will be cut as you specified.
- Select IMAGE and scroll down to SIZE. Make sure your graphic is no bigger than 4–5 inches (either width or height). The resolution should be at least 75 dpi. Improve the image by finding the options on the menu bar (this may be located on the IMAGE menu). You can adjust the image's brightness/contrast, color, and resolution, as well as the size of the photo. Some editing programs give you additional options for special effects. If you increase the amount of contrast, it can help to make text and details easier to see.
- Once you have the photo the way you want it, Select FILE from menu bar and scroll down to SAVE AS. Save the graphic as a JPEG image by clicking the down-arrow in the dialogue box under the file name. Give the image a title and make sure you record the saved name on the back of the photo along with the reference number for your bibliography.
- Click SAVE in dialogue box.

Best Tip: Don't be afraid to use the same graphic in a couple of different ways. You can crop and enlarge the same graphic to focus in on specific areas. For example, you might take a group photo, scan it as a group photo, and then crop to one person's face. Adjust the image to be at least a 3 x 5 inch canvas, and it will blow up to a full-size photo. Check to make sure the close-up is clear and does not become blurry or that it does not have large "digital" boxes (this is called pixelation). Save close-up graphic as a new JPEG image under a different name. This can add emphasis and interest and greatly increase the number of graphics you have available for creation of your video.

Learning to Use a Digital Camera

Sometimes, such as when you are at an archive, you may not be able to get a photocopy of a primary source. This is when a digital camera can be used to capture an image for your video.

A digital camera is not so different from a regular camera, except that, instead of the pictures being stored on film, they are stored on a floppy disc or a digital storage device. They also save images according to the number of pixels, or resolution. For use in a documentary, you will want to use a camera with at least a 640 x 480 resolution.

There are many brands of digital cameras. Instructions for most cameras are similar to the following:

- Turn on the power and set the camera to automatic mode. Remove the lens cap.
- Make sure you have a floppy disc or other storage device in the camera.
- Make sure that the camera is set to "Camera" instead of "Play" or "Movie."
- Put the document or photo on a flat surface and make sure that any light is soft and evenly spread over the surface of the image. Watch out that you don't get between the light and the subject, or your shadow will be on the image.
- Compose the image in the viewfinder, making sure the image that you want is in the center of the viewfinder. If you see glare, try to

reposition or move the object so that the light is less direct.

- Use the zoom feature to narrow in and get a good close-up view. If you want more of a close-up, refer to the camera manual for advice on using "macro" mode.

- Hold the camera lens at an even, parallel angle to the document or photo. Even so, you will probably see that the camera lens will tend to curve the straight lines on the edges of the image. For this reason, you will want to try to get the portion of the image that you need directly in the middle of the viewfinder.

- Hold the camera steady, bracing your elbows against your body or against the table or wall, if possible.

- Press the shutter-release button halfway down so the camera can set focus, exposure, and adjust for light.

- Press the shutter-release button all the way down to take the picture.

- To view the picture, set camera to "Play" and follow the menu. There should be an arrow up-down option that lets you view your stored images.

- If the image is not what you want, delete it and start over.

When you get back to your computer, load the images into your photo editing program and crop and adjust as needed. Print out a hard copy, indicating the name under which you saved the image on the back of the copy. You might also want to write a short caption describing the who, what, when, and where of the image.

More on Analysis

Historians interpret and analyze data that they have collected. This means that you must take the information you have gathered and *do something original with it.* Some ways to do analysis on topics include:

Compare and contrast: If there is an issue involved with your topic (there almost always is), state both sides of the issue (pro and con) and take a stand. Tell what you believe and why, based on the evidence.

Cause and effect: Explain why you believe event(s) occurred, based on the evidence, and what impact the event(s) had on history.

Acknowledging different points of view: Historians almost always differ in their interpretation of event(s). Acknowledge the different interpretations and take a stand, based on the evidence. If you've uncovered something new, say so!

Acknowledging deficiencies in the historical record: If you couldn't find evidence on a certain area related to your topic, state what is missing. For example, "The impact of the antirent wars may never be fully understood because a fire in the New York State Capitol destroyed most of the historical evidence. From what remains, we know . . . "

Historical Surveys: Survey experts, citizens, or others who have an opinion about your topic or who are first-hand observers of your event. Present the survey information in an easily readable form like a graph or pie chart. Make surveys simple—keep them limited to a few questions, provide criteria for answering (like a one-to-five scale, for example), and make sure the questions are easily understood. Make sure your survey provides meaningful information.

Graphs and charts: Take information you have gathered and create a statistical analysis of the impact of your topic on a population segment (for example, age, gender, location, ethnicity). You could graph population or environmental changes or any other statistics. Use Microsoft Excel or other spreadsheet software to create the graphs or charts.

Example of a Survey

1. Did you live during the Great Depression that began in 1929?

   Yes   No

2. How old were you at the time?

   Toddler   Child   Teen   Young Adult

3. On a scale of 1–5, please rate how the depression affected your family:

   1 = no effect   2 = mild effect   3 = moderate effect
   4 = severe effect 5 = survival threatened

Food	1	2	3	4	5
Living Conditions	1	2	3	4	5
Health	1	2	3	4	5
Employment	1	2	3	4	5

Step 5

Using the Internet for Historical Research

Using the Internet

The Internet is a wonderful tool for communication and research. Learning the basics can help you to begin exploring the world of information that is available. You would not believe the world of primary source documents that are available on the Internet! By your target date, you should have explored a *minimum* of six Internet sites.

The Internet links your computer (via a modem) with servers that link you to other servers and computers around the world, all at the touch of a button. You begin by getting access to a computer that is linked to a server (like America Online, for example) either at home or through your school or public library. The server is linked to the Internet, either through a network within the school or library or through a modem on the computer. Each server uses what is called a *browser*, which is a device that allows you to search the Internet and connect to specific pages.

Search Engines

A search engine is a web site that is designed to allow you to search for a specific subject, name, phrase, or keyword(s). Some common search engines include the following:

- Yahoo! (http://www.yahoo.com);
- AltaVista (http://www.altavista.com);
- Lycos (http://www.lycos.com); and
- Dog Pile (http://www.dogpile.com).

To connect to a search engine, you type the address into the URL box at the top of your screen (after you have been connected to the server) and either click enter or "Go." When the search engine page appears, type your search phrase into the box and click "Go" or "Search." You will then see a page appear that has a list of "hits" that match your search phrase. The links will take you to the appropriate page once you have clicked your mouse on top of the web address. These hits are web sites that include your keyword or phrase somewhere within the contents of the page. Sites that seem to match your inquiry most closely are listed first. Be careful! A search gives you any site, accurate or inaccurate, that relates to your search phrase.

Know the Author

When you are researching, it is important that you know the source of information you are gathering. The Internet is a great resource tool, but it is vital to remember that anyone can put up a web page containing information. Just like in real life, pages reflect the opinions, prejudices, and inaccuracies of human beings. Recently, a professor at a major university discovered that a history site with thousands of "primary sources" was actually loaded with errors. Documents had been invented and others had been changed in order to make history agree with the perspectives of the person who created the web site and to sell a book that the person had written. Evaluate each Internet site carefully. Is anyone trying to sell you something? What are the objectives of the designer? To help you sort out the good from the bad, know the meanings of the "domains," which are the abbreviations in the web address that state what type of organization is putting the page on the web.

Common Domain Names

- .com is a commercial organization, organized to make a profit
- .gov is a governmental agency
- .edu is an educational institution
- .org is a nonprofit organization
- .int is an international organization
- .net is a networking organization

Search Tips

To search for a keyword, just type it in. If you want to search for a phrase like a title, place it in quotes, otherwise the search engine will search for each word independently and give you hits that include any of the words in any combination. If you want two words together, but not necessarily following each other, use a plus (+) sign between the words. Some search engines (like AltaVista) allow you to do specialized searches for images (photos), sounds, or video files. On AltaVista, just click on the menu tab above the search box for the type of information you would like. If you are unable to find what you are searching for by using one search engine, try again with a different search engine. Very often, you will find a large difference in the hits that are produced.

Investigating Hits

Before you start wildly clicking your mouse on top of the links that appear, do some detective work on the results page the search engine presents you. Look at the address and check the domain information. If you see ".com," it's a clue that there might have been a financial incentive or business reason for putting the information on the Internet. If you see

".edu," look for initials of a university or college within the web address. Excellent historical sites can be found at many of our nation's university libraries or archives. Some search engines present the first sentence as it appears on the web page. Does this give you any more clues as to the type of information presented on that site?

Important Internet Sites For History

- The *National Archives* (http://www.nara.gov) lets you search their NAIL database for digital images of primary source documents and photos, as well as nondigital information that you could use to order copies of documents. You can also find links to Presidential Libraries and some digitized exhibits. Go to the main page, click on "Research Room," and then on "Search NAIL database."

- *The Library of Congress American Memory* site (http://memory.loc.gov) gives access to primary source documents and has a wonderful collection of oral histories and digitized film and music from the early part of the century.

- *History Net* (http://www.thehistorynet.com/home.htm) gives you access to many, many documents and history links.

- *Athens Forum* (http://www.geocities.com:80/Athens/Forum/9061/USA/twenty/twenty.html) has links to a number of sites dealing with the 20th century.

- *Rutgers University* (http://www.libraries.rutgers.edu) has one of the best collections of primary documents for the Civil War. Go to the main page and click on "Search Library Websites."

- *WWII Sounds and Pictures* (http://www.earthstation1.simplenet.com/wwii.html) offers recordings and images from the second world war.

- *Time Magazine* (http://www.thepicturecollection.com) gives free access (registration is necessary) to 20 million photos from 1930 to the present.

- *Brigham Young University* (http://www.lib.byu.edu/~rdh/wwi) has a digitized collection of primary sources dealing with World War I.

- *NASA* (http://www.hq.nasa.gov) gives access to many primary sources on space exploration, including Apollo missions.

- *The Franklin and Eleanor Roosevelt Institute* (http://www.newdeal. feri.org) and the *FDR Presidential Library* (http://www.academic. marist.edu/fdr) contain links to New Deal information. Over 10,000 digitized documents are available.
- *Historical Photos Online* (http://www.ucr.edu/h-gig/hist-art/photo.html).
- *University of Virginia's* (http://www.lib.virginia.edu/exhibits/ lewis_clark/home.html) exhibit on Monticello and Lewis and Clark has primary source maps and documents.
- *Yale University's Avalon Site* (http://www.yale.edu/lawweb/avalon/ wwii/wwii.htm) gives lots of documents on World War II. If you have difficulty accessing this site, go to a search engine (like www.yahoo.com) and type in search phrase "Avalon +Project +Yale."
- Excellent old movie footage on hundreds of topics, including cold war bomb drills in schools and immigration (www.moviearchive. org/movie/index.html).
- *New York State Archives (*http://www.sara.nysed.gov).

Directions for Saving From the Internet (PC)

Saving Text

- Highlight the section that you would like to save.
- Pull down the Edit Menu and choose COPY.
- Minimize the screen by clicking on the box with the line in the upper right-hand corner.
- Click on your word-processing program icon— usually Microsoft Word or Corel Word Perfect.
- Open a new document.
- Pull down Edit Menu and choose PASTE.
- Fill in the bibliographic form and type in the source number you gave the site, underlined, two lines under your notes—then skip two more lines. This will tell you where you found the information later on.
- To go back to Internet, minimize the document and click on the Internet box at bottom of screen.

- When done taking notes, go to FILE and Click SAVE AS. When the screen comes up, make sure the top box indicates you are saving to FLOPPY A drive or to the appropriate disc or network. Hit the down arrow to find other options for saving.
- Title the document and SAVE.
- Print a copy when you are done taking notes.

Saving Graphics

- Make sure you have accessed the full document, not just a thumbnail.
- Put your cursor (mouse) over the graphic you want to save.
- Right-Click with the mouse.
- When you see menu options, choose SAVE PICTURE AS.
- In top section of SAVE AS dialogue box, make sure you are saving to FLOPPY A drive or appropriate disc. Hit the down arrow in the box to get other options.

> **Thumbnail:** Very small image, kind of an index of what is available. If you click on the thumbnail, you usually access the larger , higher quality image.

- In bottom section, name the graphic.
- In bottom section, try to save as a JPEG (preferable). Sometimes the JPEG option is not available. Of other options, Bitmap is preferable to GIF. Hit the down-arrow to find other options. Try not to save as an "art" file because these usually do not import into other programs very well. Click SAVE.
- Print out a copy for your photograph file and bibliography information. Indicate on the back of the copy the name and file location under which you have saved the image.

Step 6

Write
for Information

Guide to Writing Research Letters

ne way to obtain research materials for your project is to write to associations, museums, government agencies, libraries, colleges, or experts that have information on your topic.

Where can I find addresses of people to write to for information?

Many times you can find e-mail or regular mail addresses on the Internet. Use a search engine to search for keywords related to your topic (see "Searching the Internet"). You might also try adding the word museum or association to your keyword. Don't forget to search for government agencies that might be related to your topic. Use the search engine's people finder to search for authors of books or magazine articles on your topic or names of key people that you have come across in your research. If a bibliography in one of the books you located mentions that a primary source was located in a college or university library, do a search for the university's home page and find the link to their library. Librarians will often be willing to send you information. You could also try the *Encyclopedia of Associations*, *Encyclopedia of Museums*, or a similar reference book that lists special-interest organizations.

How Do I Write the Letter or E-mail?

There are some rules for writing good requests for information:

Salutation

A good letter or e-mail begins with "Dear," followed by the name of the person to whom you are writing. If you don't know a person's name (for example, if you are writing to a museum), then address it "To Whom It May Concern."

Always identify yourself and your reason for writing.

Example: "My name is Joe Blake, and I am a student at Whichitawa Middle School, Springfield, NY. I am creating a documentary on President Kennedy for my history class."

Briefly ask some specific questions.

Keep your questions *very focused and direct*. (A good rule is to limit yourself to three or four of your most important questions). Busy people will not have time to search through an entire collection or library for you.

Ask very pointed research questions or, if you're asking for information to be sent to you, explain what you would like to receive. If you want a phone interview, ask for an appointment or a time that you can call them and the phone number at which they can be reached. Offer to pay for any copying expenses for documents that might be sent to you.

Tip: Do not ask for "Everything you know about . . ." or "Everything you have on . . ." *Just asking for information on your broad topic will not work!* Sometimes there are hundreds of boxes of archived files that relate to a broad topic. Also, remember that an archive, museum, or library may have many requests. The more specific you are, the more likely it is that you will find a package of information in the mail.

Example: "I've done some background reading on President Kennedy's contributions to the NASA program. I was wondering if you could help me locate some primary sources for my research.

- Could you please send me a copy of JFK's "Race for Space" speech?
- Do you know where I could find photos of JFK at NASA or with astronauts?
- What do you think was the biggest influence on JFK's determination to advance the U.S. space program?
- Can you suggest any other places where I could find primary documents or an expert I could interview?

I will be glad to pay for the cost of any copying or postage."

Let the person know where and how they can contact you.
Example: "You can reach me by e-mail at ICanDoThis.freenet.com. Materials can be sent to my home at 123 Goodbook Lane, Whichimata, NY 11113."

Tell the person what kind of deadline you are working under.
Example: "The project must be finished by the first week of March, when it has to be presented to my social studies class."

Thank them.
Example: "Thank you for your time. This means a lot to me."

Close with a signature:
Sincerely, yours truly, or so on.

Example of a Research Request

Joe Blake
123 Goodbook Lane
Whichimata, NY 11113

October 21, 2000

Library
Baseball Hall of Fame
Cooperstown, NY

To whom it may concern:

My name is Joe Blake, and I am doing a research project for National History Day. I am a sixth-grade student at Whichimata Middle School in Whichimata, NY. My topic is on Babe Ruth, and the theme for the contest this year is "Turning Points in History." I would like to show how turning points in Babe Ruth's life led to his great career.

I have done some background reading and had a few questions that I thought you might be able to help me with:

What was the name of Babe Ruth's first coach?
Are there any letters or other documents that would help me describe what the "turning point" was in Babe Ruth's life?
Do you know where I could find photographs of Babe Ruth as a teenager?
Do you know of an expert on Babe Ruth who I might be able to interview?

You can write me at the above address or e-mail me at jblake@yahoo.com. I will be glad to pay for any copying or mailing expenses. The project must be completed by the first week of March, in time for the regional contest.

Thank you for your help.

Step 7

Broaden Your Historical Research With Databases, Newspapers, and Periodicals

No, you're not done with your research yet! After you have written letters requesting information, it is time to search for more primary and secondary sources using databases and then search for other periodicals or newspapers. Databases, periodicals, and microfilm copies of old newspapers are usually available at large public or college/university libraries.

A database is a way of collecting and organizing data so that the user can easily search for and access information. There are different types of databases. One of the most common is a computerized library catalogue. Many databases allow for keyword searches of periodicals. One common database is the MAS Online Plus from EBSCOhost, which gives access to full-text articles from 325 magazines. Included in that database is an especially useful magazine for history research, the *Essential Documents of American History*, and it allows the printing of full-text primary source documents, as well as historical photographs. Check with school, public library, or college/university libraries to see if they can give you access to this valuable database. Access MAS by following these instructions:

- Follow the library's directions for accessing databases. Click on *EBSCOhost Web*, then click on *MAS Online Plus*.
- You will see a search box for subject and another for magazine title. Type in your keyword(s) in the subject box, then type in

"**Essential Documents**" in the box for magazine title. Your search phrase should be general in nature. Click search.

- On slower computers, sometimes MAS has a tendency to freeze. If this happens, click the STOP button on your browser once. Do not click REFRESH.
- You will see a listing of documents for your keyword. Click on any link to bring up full-text articles and documents. Magazine articles do not, however, have photos attached. For this reason, it is probably best to look at the periodical itself if you can find a copy. Write down the reference and then refer to "Periodical Search" on the next page.
- To search for photos, click the button for **image collection** located on the menu bar at the top of the screen, and then select **Historical Photos**.
- Type in your keyword and search again for images.
- If you do not get results with your search phrase, try other variations or spellings of the keyword(s). A search for "atom bomb," for example, brought up no hits, but when "atomic bomb" was entered, there were quite a few.

SIRS Researcher is another database that is often available at schools and public libraries. This is a resource that gives full-text articles and documents that are related to social issues like the environment, genetics, and the death penalty.

Now, it is time to search for periodical articles using the information you gathered from your EBSCO (MAS) or other periodicals database search. Periodical databases are usually limited in the number of years that are indexed. EBSCOhost, for example, only goes back about 10 years. For that reason, it is recommended that you do a personal search of the printed digests that list all articles ever published in a specific time period. To be effective in this, you must use your background research of your topic to pinpoint year(s) or specific dates for searching.

Some publications print digests that list all of the articles that have ever been published within the publication since it began. *National Geographic* has a wonderful index, as does *American Heritage*. Ask the librarian what digests are available. You could also try a search of *The*

Reader's Guide to Periodical Literature. This is an index that is published on a yearly basis, so you should have a year in mind to search. For example, if you know that the Love Canal disaster happened during the early 1970s, you could do a yearly search for your keywords using the Readers' Guide from those years.

Newspapers

You can also search microfilmed copies of newspapers like the *New York Times.* Either look up a specific date (month, day, year) that you know is associated with your event or topic, or look at the yearly published index and search for your keywords. Issues of the *New York Times* are available on microfilm in most major public or college/university libraries. Microfilm is read on a machine called a "microfilm reader" by loading the reel of film onto spools. The spools turn, winding the film under a lens. The lens magnifies the image, and in some cases also turns it from a negative image (white-on-black) to a positive image (black-on-white) for reading. Ask the librarian to give you a demonstration on how to lead and operate the reader. Some libraries also require you to do a search to find the page number of the specific article on one type of reader before moving to the type of reader that allows you to make photocopies of the article. When you print out photocopies, note the name of the newspaper, date of the article, and page number of the article on the back of the copy. You will need this for your bibliography.

Step 8

Search for Video Footage

Every documentary needs some live footage, preferably primary source footage, to add interest. You will be filming interviews and possibly doing on-location shooting in the next step; however, you can also use some clips from professional video productions and historic footage found in video libraries.

Begin by searching your library catalogue for videos listed under your keywords. Also, ask your teacher if the school has a special catalogue or library for videotapes and obtain copies of any that deal with your topic. Keep records in your bibliography form and note any primary source clips you might like to use.

You can also do a search of a public or university library that carries videotapes, or even check local video rental stores. Look for professional documentaries on your time period or topic. For example, a History Channel documentary on New York City might have clips about a more specific topic. You might find clips about a specific battle in documentaries about World War II. Only use clips that show primary footage, not historical reenactments.

Occasionally, with a late-20th-century topic (1960 to present), television station archives may be able to help you get footage. Either call the station yourself, or ask your teacher for assistance.

CD software can also be a good source of primary footage that has already been digitized. For a recent video project, students used primary footage of the New York City garment industry in 1903 that was taken from a Smithsonian Institution CD. Check out the CD section in your school's computer room. A very good source is the *Laser Disc Encyclopedia of the 20th Century*. Ask your librarian if your school carries this reference work or something similar to it. If not, check with local university or college libraries, but first ask the librarian if the media room can allow you to copy the laser disc footage to VHS tape.

Over the past two years, there has been an explosion in the quantity of primary source film and video that is available on the web because of the development of *streaming technology. Streaming video* is a succession of "moving images," and *streaming media* also includes sound. These images and/or sounds are sent in condensed (compressed) form over the Internet and displayed on your computer by the use of software called a *player.* The player expands the condensed data into a readable form and plays it on your monitor and/or speakers. Basic versions of common readers like Real Player and Window's Media Player are available on the Internet for free. Look for a link on the page that offers the streaming media, or go to http://www.real.com or http://www. microsoft.com/windows/windowsmedia/en/download. Two places with streaming historical footage are the American Memory collection of the Library of Commerce, (http://memory.loc.gov), and the extensive collection at (http://www.moviearchive.org/movie/index.html). Also try a keyword search at AltaVista (http://www.altavista.com) by clicking the link for "media/topic search" and then clicking the circle for video footage. You can adjust your browser to download the video directly to your hard drive. If this is not possible, then you can set the player to play at full-screen and export the movie to a VCR for recording.

Be creative in looking for footage—don't forget libraries and museums, which will often let you borrow copies of videotapes. Ask the experts you have contacted where you can find primary source footage on videotape.

Note: By U.S. copyright law (unless a source is in the public domain), up to 10%, or three minutes (whichever is less), of video media may be copied for educational use without asking permission of the copyright holder. It is best not to "copy" stills that have been shot professionally, however, because you should be getting access to those photos and either shooting them yourself or digitizing them by scanning. Avoid using interview segments that have been created for professional documentaries. It is much better to schedule your own interview for your project. Basically, what you are looking for is *primary source film footage.* Don't waste your three minutes of copyright privilege on something you can create for yourself.

When you find video footage, it is important that you "log" the data so that the clips you need will be easy to find when you transfer them to your documentary. To do this, you need a VCR with an accurate counter.

- Make a copy of the video logging master form.
- Log each VHS tape separately.
- Reset the VCR counter to "00000" at the start of logging each separate VHS tape.
- Start the VHS tape by hitting "Play."
- When you see a clip you think you might like to use in your documentary, rewind to the beginning of the clip.
- Record the count number in the "time in" box of the log.
- Play the clip to the end, recording the count number in the "time out" box.
- Also, record the subject of the clip on the log.
- Do this for each separate clip on the same video before resetting the counter to zero. You may want to put a star next to especially important clips.

Videotape Log

Title of Videotape	Action or Subject of Clip	Time In on VCR Counter	Time Out on VCR Counter

Step 9

Film or Tape Oral History Interviews

How to Conduct an Oral History Interview

By now, you should already have at least one or two interviews scheduled. Learning to do a successful interview is easy. Just follow the tips in this chapter and you'll be able to get the most out of your interviews.

Pitfalls

Please understand that, although an interview is considered a primary source if the subject actually experienced events covered by your topic, there are some drawbacks to relying completely on evidence supplied by interviews. Memories can be faulty, especially if they go back over a long period of time. Personal prejudices can affect the way people interpret events and facts. A large percentage of interview is therefore considered opinion, not absolute fact.

Benefits

There is nothing like talking to a person who experienced history first-hand. It can give a depth of understanding and a personal dimension that is needed to give life to history. Quality documentaries need the drama and special flavor that personal perspectives can give to topics.

Tips and Techniques for a Successful Interview

Write your questions ahead of time. You *must* do background reading before the interview so that you can ask intelligent questions about the topic. Some questioning strategies include:

- Establish at the beginning of the interview who the person is, what his or her role was in the event, and how he or she was an eyewitness to history. (If they are a secondary source, How he or she is an expert on the topic).
- Do not ask yes-or-no questions! Ask open-ended questions that encourage the interview subject to tell his or her story. Ask questions that require an *in-depth answer.*

Have a talk with the interview subject before the interview date. Tell his or her the kinds of questions you will most likely ask and about how much time the interview will take. Tell him or her the interview will be taped and whether or not it will be recorded on video. Confirm the arrangements (time, date, place) for the interview.

Bring recording devices with you. Check out your equipment beforehand to make sure you know how it works. Make sure you try out the video camera and microphone ahead of time (see tips on page 72), understand where to plug it in, and so forth. Practice on someone at home before you go to the interview. Play it back and see if you can figure out how to do it even better. If you are interviewing by phone, obtain an inexpensive device that hooks up your telephone to your tape recorder. If you are interviewing by phone, make sure you inform the interview subject that he or she is being taped!

Have conversational icebreakers in mind, especially for the beginning of the interview. Part of your job is to put the interview subject at ease and help him or her overcome nervousness. *Relax! If you are nervous, your interview subject will be nervous, also.*

Relax, and let the interview occur naturally. Put your interview subject at ease by having a friendly conversation beforehand. Tell him or her about your topic, what you have discovered so far, and so forth.

During the interview,

- Go with your prepared questions, but do not feel that you have to stick only to the questions you've already written. Listen to the answers the subject gives you and make sure you ask intelligent follow-up questions. Consider interesting responses as your "leads" to additional questions.
- Don't rush through the questions! Take your time.
- Listen to the silence. Don't feel awkward and rush ahead when there is not an immediate response . . . the subject may be pondering how to respond. Let him or her fill the silence.
- Ask probing questions . . . in addition to who, what, when, and where; ask why and how often. Ask for opinions and reflections. If you are entering a competition, ask how the subject feels the topic relates to the contest theme. For example: "How do you think the bombing of Pearl Harbor was a turning point in history?" Even if you think you already know the answer, getting an interview subject to state it might be helpful as a sound byte or quote.
- Do not ask leading questions. Leading questions tell what you think the correct answer is and might prejudice the interviewee into giving you the answer you are expecting, instead of his or her own opinion.
- Ask well-thought-out questions. Don't try to mix up five questions in one! In general, a brief question is better than a long one because it is easier for the interviewee to understand what the interviewer is asking.

- Don't interrupt a good story because you suddenly thought of a question. Bring a small notebook with you and jot down your question so you can ask it later.

After the interview, make sure you thank the person and then send him or her a thank-you letter within five days after the close of the interview. You might need further information from him or her later on—don't make the interviewer feel that you were ungrateful for his or her assistance!

Tips for Recording a Videotaped Interview

Tip #1: Play with the camcorder and microphone before the interview date. Make sure you know how the microphone plugs into the camcorder. Practice focusing and zooming. Hit RECORD and STOP. Make sure you are comfortable and self-confident of your ability to work the camcorder.

Tip #2: Limit the movement in the shot. Bring a tripod with you and secure the camcorder in one spot. Do not move the camcorder or zoom in during the interview.

Tip #3: Use a unidirectional microphone for best sound. Do not rely on the camcorder's built-in microphone. Unidirectional microphones help to filter out background noise and focus on the subject. Even so, try to eliminate background noise by setting up in the quietest spot you can find.

Tip #4: Take your time setting up the shot. Make sure that you take a "head-shot" (from shoulders up) and center the person in the screen. Interview subjects are commonly known as "talking heads" because of this common set-up for the shot.

Camera Tip: Observe the "Rule of Thirds." Make sure the eyes of your talking head are approximately one-third of the way from the top of your shot.

Tip #5: After the interview is over, take some cutaway shots. If the talking head referred to an object during the interview, take a close or macro shot of it after the interview is complete.

Tip #6: What if your talking head isn't talking? If you have an interview subject who is talking like a chatterbox before you tape, then gives you only short answers when being taped, he or she is probably camera-shy. One trick (a bit sneaky, but it works!) is to pretend you are turning the camera off, but then leave it on. Come out from behind the camera a bit, but stay situated so that the interview subject is facing the direction of the camera. Be as relaxed as you can and begin talking with the person instead of firing questions at him or her. You will probably get some usable sound bytes this way. For ethical reasons, after the interview is over, you should tell the subject what you did and why. He or she may want to see the footage to make sure there is nothing he or she told you that he or she would prefer to keep off the record.

Project Check

Group or Individual Name(s):

At this stage, it helps to assess your work so that you know you are on the way to a quality product. Be honest, so that you can receive help as needed. Complete this form and hand it in to your teacher.

Answer the following questions by checking the appropriate column:

Effort in each research area was . . .	Outstanding	Average	Poor	Not Done
Well-written notes on content from at least two secondary books on topic. Notes develop a timeline of events, answer research questions, and establish historical context/time period of topic.				
Well-written notes on topic taken from at least one general reference work or encyclopedia. Notes answer "who, what, when, where, and why."				
Analysis of at least a dozen primary source documents on topic and notes on what was learned from each. Notes on quotations or facts from primary sources for possible use in script.				
Internet search and printing of primary sources on topic. Photographs printed in hard copy for photo file and saved to floppy disc or network drive, with notation of saved name on printed copy.				
Two letters written for information on topic. Questions in letters were focused and asked for specific assistance or information.				
Periodical indexes or databases searched. Articles printed or copied and/or saved to floppy disc. Photographs saved to floppy disc with printed copy for photo file. Saved name noted on copy.				
Videos on topic located and viewed. Possible clips to use in product logged on form. Video clips from Internet saved on disc or printed to VHS tape. Music appropriate to time period or topic located and noted.				
Interview subjects located. Videotaped interviews conducted with expert on topic or eyewitness to event. Tape logged on form to indicate sound bytes for possible use in product.				
Photo/Graphic file is up-to-date. Notes on back of each copy are written in pencil and note bibliographic source number, caption info, and names under which graphic is saved on computer.				
Bibliographic information is up-to-date. Each source has been assigned a number. Analysis of each source written in annotation. Coordination with all members of group.				
All members of group have coordinated and shared information, especially with bibliography sources. Time has been used effectively.				

Assistance is needed with: _____

Step 10

Writing
the Script

Congratulations! You have finished the research phase and are ready to begin creating your product. If you are working in a group, you should refocus by making a change in group roles (see handout).

Steps in Writing the Script

Create an Outline

The first step in writing a script is to create an outline on the information you have learned during research. Think of this as a preliminary step to a research report. Start with an introduction, followed by some background information on the historical period in which the event(s) occurred. You may also want to explain the geographic location of the events. Next, add a chronological outline of the events that relate to your topic. Give an account of what occurred and why it is important.

Chronological: Arranged in or according to the order of time

This skeleton outline would look something like the example below from a student-created documentary on the Triangle Shirtwaist Fire:

I.   Introduction
II.   Background of the 1900 era
    A. Immigration
    B. Garment industry employment
    C. Labor movements & strike
III. Conditions in Triangle Factory
    A. Locked doors
    B. Not enough fire escapes
IV.   Fire & Deaths
    A. How and when fire started
    B. Rescue efforts
    C. Fire escape breaking
    D. People jumping
    E. Death count
V.   Memorial meeting/Public outrage after the fire
VI.   Factory investigating commission
VII. Fire as a turning point
    A. Bills produced by Factory Investigating Commission
VIII. Sweatshops today
IX.   Conclusion

Next, you need to "flesh out" the skeleton by writing the introduction and conclusion and then filling in specific details. Choose quotes and facts and use them to fill in the details of the events. It would be helpful at this point to word-process your script because it will be easier to make changes to the work while it is in progress.

A good documentary develops the important aspects of the topic as fully as possible. Time limits, however, will require using good judgment as to which quotes and facts are essential to include and which details can be eliminated without getting in the way of the audience's understanding of the topic. Look over all of the research that you have accumulated and choose the facts and quotations that will tell the story of events. Fit these into the proper place and use them to develop your outline into a script.

Review the videotaped interviews for clips that will help develop the story of events.

You also want your documentary to have emotional impact that will involve the viewer. Try to make the people who are involved come to life as much as possible by choosing quotes that have both historical significance and a depth of feeling. Tell a story! Use all the good elements of storytelling—description, setting, characterization—to make the audience care about the people who were involved. An example of this is the group that wrote a boring first script on child labor that was filled with census statistics and a factual accounting of laws. To bring their script to life, they introduced the audience to a real child they had read about in a newspaper article. The article they found gave few details about the mills, so the group used facts and quotations from oral histories to tell about conditions in a typical clothing mill of the time period. This helped them to create an account of what the child's average day might have been like. They took the audience step-by-step through the workday of this 10-year-old, describing in detail his day from the time he woke up in his family's tenement, to the point where he was killed while cleaning one of the weaving machines.

Don't forget to be a historian. It is your job to interpret and analyze history. Tell what impact the event(s) you discuss had on history. What causes and effects have you discovered? How has the topic changed our world or society? Historians often use some of the following phrases when they analyze events:

- *Experts have long thought that, but our (my) research leads to the conclusion that . . .*
- *Historians disagree on . . . but we (I) think that . . . because . . .*
- *Careful study of the documents reveals that . . .*
- *One possible cause for this might have been . . .*
- *We (I) were (was) surprised that . . .*
- *It could be that . . .*

You get the idea. Tell what you think! Back up your conclusions with evidence! If you uncovered something new, say so, and tell how this might change the interpretation of events. Always refer to evidence or the "why" of what led you to your conclusions.

Transitions

The last step in writing a script is to check all segments of the script to make sure each section of information blends well, each leading the audience to the next piece of information. A script should flow easily and lead the audience slowly, instead of jumping quickly from one subtopic to another. Some words and phrases that will help to create good transitions are:

Immediately	*Meanwhile*	*At the same time,*
On the other hand	*Nevertheless*	*For example*
Consequently	*As a result*	*For instance*
The change was	*Instead of*	*After a short time*
Months later	*Specifically*	

Introduction and Conclusion

The introduction and conclusion are perhaps two of the most important segments of your video. The introduction will lead the audience into your topic and let them know what your documentary will prove or show. If you are entering a competition, you will probably want to tell how the topic relates to the contest theme. The conclusion will be a summary that wraps up with your thoughts about the topic's importance. What have you proved? What meaning or significance does this piece of history have for us today? What words of wisdom related to the topic (this could be a quotation) are important for the world to remember?

Group Roles During Production (Nonlinear Desktop Editing)

Writer(s)

- Writes and word-processes script, conferencing with other group members for input.
- With other members of group, creates storyboard, choosing quotations and statistics for script.
- Writes effective transitions that tie each part of the script together.
- Changes script as needed during editing process.

Media Technician

- With other group members, decides which video clips are needed for documentary and creates storyboard.
- Serves as cameraperson during filming.
- Takes digital photographs as needed.
- Imports and captures analog or digital footage into editing software, trimming for use.
- Renders (produces) video by using software features.
- Outputs video to VHS tape, printing as many copies as needed.

Graphic Design Technician

- With other group members, decides which photos and graphic images are needed for documentary and creates storyboard.
- Scans photographs, graphics, and documents for use in documentary.
- Imports photographs, graphics, and documents into editing software.
- As needed, makes adjustments to graphic images using photo editing or video editing software.
- Titles video and interview clips.
- Creates title screen and credits.

Editor

- Places digitized images and video clips in sequence in storyboard within editing software program.

- Assists sound technician in timing images and sequences to narration.
- Times overall length of documentary, trimming narration or script as necessary.
- Adds transitions and other special effects as necessary.

Sound Technician

- With other group members, decides what audio is needed for documentary and creates storyboard.
- Assigns parts of narration to group members.
- Captures narration and other audio, trimming to fit graphic image.
- Keeps list of the file names attached to clip narrations and records file names on script.
- Plays back each clip, making sure sound is of high quality.
- Captures background music and trims to fit clips within documentary.
- Adds sound effects or other audio as necessary.
- Mixes audio with video images.

Group Roles During Production
(Linear Assemble or In-Camera Editing)

Writer(s)

- Writes and word-processes script, conferencing with other group members for input.
- With other group members, creates storyboard, choosing quotations and statistics for script.
- Writes effective transitions that tie each part of the script together.
- Changes script as needed during editing process.

Media Technician

- With other group members, decides which video clips are needed for documentary and creates storyboard.
- Serves as cameraperson during filming of still images and location shots. *Films in order* of the storyboard.

Graphic Design Technician

- With other group members, decides which photos and graphic images are needed for documentary, and creates storyboard.
- Creates title screen and credits and gives them to Media Technician for filming.

Sound Technician

- With other group members, decides what audio is needed for documentary and helps to create storyboard.
- Assigns parts of narration to group members and rehearses their reading of the script.
- After a master video has been produced, uses camcorder's audio dub feature to record narration.
- Chooses background music and plays it in background during recording and audio dub.
- Plays back each clip, making sure sound is of high quality.

Editor

- Times overall length of documentary, trimming narration or script as necessary.
- Uses assemble editing to arrange visuals and insert interview(s), primary source footage, or location shots and creates a master tape.
- Assists sound technician in audio dubbing of narration and background music.
- Adds transitions and other special effects as necessary.

Step 11

Storyboarding

nce the script has been written, it is time to storyboard your documentary. During this step, you use special forms (or index cards) to match visual images with the script narration. A master storyboard form is provided.

Storyboard: A series of panels on which a set of sketches is arranged in order to show the important changes of scene and action (as for a film, television show, or commercial)

Begin this step by reviewing the photographs, graphics, and video clips that were accumulated during research. A copy of the script should be in front of you as you look for visuals that can illustrate various sections. When you find a visual you feel is appropriate for a section, fill in the visual image section of the form with stick figures. You could also simply list a name you assigned to the photo.

In the audio section, abbreviate by writing the first couple of words from the script second, then ". . . ," and the last couple of words from the section. In the section for music/other, list background music, sound effects, or type of camera movement (i.e. zoom, pan) that is needed to emphasize the visual.

The script segments should be matched with a visual at least every 8, but no more than 12 seconds, (unless it is moving footage). It takes about seven seconds for the human brain to understand what it is seeing and match the information with the audio being heard. After about 11 seconds, the viewer is ready to move on to new information.

The type of visuals you use should be varied as much as possible. Use clips from primary source film footage and your oral history interviews to create movement in your video. Vary the types of shots (wide, medium, close) to create impact. Decide which visuals can be presented as still shots and which need camera movement for enhancement, and write down this information in the music/other section.

An example storyboard and matching page of script are provided on the following pages. Following the example is a master storyboard form. **Do not write on the master.** Copy it as needed.

Example of a Page of a Script and Accompanying Storyboard

Script written by Henna Boolchandani, Sara Chmielewski, Christine Groat, Christine Meglino, and Erin Parks
First Place Winners, Jr. Group Documentary Division, New York State Finals, National History Day, 2000

SCRIPT REVISION 4/28

TITLE SCREEN WITH FIREFIGHTER PICTURE   8 seconds
   "Tragedy in a Factory" Scroll
   Names Scroll

INTRODUCTION   (Filmed live at Labor Department)   32 seconds

Today, state and federal labor departments protect workers from safety and health hazards. In 1911, however, there was no separate federal labor agency, and the New York State Labor Department was weak and had little power to enforce regulations. The fledgling agency got a much-needed "boost" when a tragic event transpired. On March 25, 1911, a blazing fire broke out in the Triangle Shirtwaist factory building, taking the lives of 146 innocent people. Their deaths inspired a turning point in history.

SHIP   (Still)   9 seconds

In the early 1900s over a million immigrants came to America each year with high hopes of starting a new life.

IMMIGRANTS (Still)   4 seconds

SMALL FAMILY (Zoom in to close shot from Immigrants wide shot)   6 seconds

What they found was not the glorious dream they had hoped for, but instead they were trapped in a world of poverty. Over half of them lived in crowded, unsanitary tenements.

SMITHSONIAN FILM OF CLOTHING FACTORY   14 seconds

Many immigrants worked in the garment industry, in what were called sweatshops. Ruthless factory owners could easily take advantage of vulnerable workers who were desperate to make a living.

LITTLE CHILDREN (Still)   12 seconds

Conditions in sweatshops were appalling. Even children as young as 8 were forced to work in tight, crammed workrooms. Workers, the majority of them women, labored from 8–15 hours a day.

	Visual Image	Narration	Music/Other
Shot #	Firefighters (Graphic #10)	NONE	Fire.wav, as TRAGEDY IN A FACTORY scrolls. BY (Scroll Names) Henna Boolchandani Christine Groat Christine Meglino Erin Parks Sara Chmielewski
☐	NYS Dept LaborWIDE Shot, ZOOM to Medium	"Today, state and... ... point in history."	NONE Camera zooms to medium Shot of Christine
☐	CROWDED SHIP Still (Graphic #4)	"In the early 1900's... ...new life"	Legend of 1900 CD cut 8 start low + ↑volume
☐	Immigrants graphic #22 (zoom in to SMALL family on Left)	"What they found... ...world of poverty."	Continue music on Med. vol. Zoom into family

Media Storyboard

Media Storyboard		

	Visual Image	Narration	Music/Other
Shot #			
☐			
☐			
☐			
☐			

87

Choosing Background Music for Your Documentary

Choosing appropriate background music for your documentary is crucial to the development of a professional production. It sets the mood, establishes the time era, and highlights important segments of the script. There are some important principles to keep in mind:

- **Choose music that is appropriate for the time period and/or emotional feel of your subject.** For example, swing music or the big band sound would be appropriate music for a World War II-era documentary, but you would not want to use a sound that is extremely peppy and upbeat on a portion of your video where you discuss casualties (deaths in battle). You could still use the big band sound for your introduction and/or credits, and then switch to a slower paced, more somber piece for the appropriate clips.

- **If editing on computer, find music on CD-ROM.** This is the easiest to import into the computer.

- **Make sure the background music for sections of your video where you have narration or other sound is an instrumentals-only music selection.** You don't want lyrics to interfere with other sound and take attention away from the narration or interview.

- **If in doubt, choose a classical piece of music.** These almost always work well with any topic.

- **Beware of choosing music that is being played currently on the radio or on MTV.** If a piece is too identifiable with the present time, it might distract attention from the historical feel that you are trying to create.

- **Make sure your music piece is in the public domain.** Educational use is limited to 30 seconds of music if it has an active copyright in force.

Public domain: Works that are free of copyright restrictions

Step 12

Camera Work

Lights, Camera, Action! Filming With a Camcorder

Now that you have completed your storyboard, you are ready to begin filming. To create a professional-quality documentary, you must observe some rules for using a camcorder. You should have already made choices about how much of the scene to include, whether to do a still shot or show movement, what angle to shoot from, and so forth.

Rule #1: Hold steady! *Always* secure the camcorder on a tripod. There is nothing worse than watching a video of unintentional shakes and tremors. Unless your topic is the San Francisco Earthquake, there is no excuse for shaky recording!

Rule #2: Focus! Take your time when setting up the shot. Focus and zoom in so that the view through the viewfinder looks just like you want it to in your video. Beware of "borders" around your shot. (See sidebar on the following page on preparing graphics for shooting.) Shoot at least one minute of black (nothing) at the beginning of each new tape before shooting because the beginning and ends of tape are more prone to get dirty

Prepare Your Graphic Before Filming!

Before shooting a graphic, cut (straight and even cut, please) carefully around the edges of the graphic, removing any border. Put masking tape on the back of the graphic and tape it to the middle of a piece of black construction paper that has been taped to the wall at camcorder height. The black border works to disguise small errors in lining up the shot and looks professional. The graphic should always be at an even height to the camera lens.

and stretch, causing static and editing problems. If you are doing assemble or in-camera editing (also called linear editing), you will have to film in order of the storyboard. See Step 13 for additional tips on linear editing.

Rule #3: Move the camera only if you have a purpose! If you are shooting a still, decide ahead of time whether you need movement and limit yourself to one type of movement in a shot (slow and steady, no in-and-out-and-in or up-and-down or else the viewer will get seasick!). Don't be afraid to shoot the same graphic in a couple of different ways. For example, you could do a shot showing the entire graphic, then stop recording, set up another shot as a close-up of a feature in the graphic, and begin shooting again. In this way, the same graphic can give you several different shots for your documentary. This is a good trick for creating drama and emphasis (imagine a war scene showing several soldiers fighting, with the next shot being a close-up of one soldier's face or hands).

Rule #4: Get clear sound! For location shoots with dialogue or interviews, use an exterior (unidirectional) microphone, not the mike on the camcorder. This way, you will get the best, broadcast-quality sound. Otherwise, it will be fuzzy or sound like you're filming in a tin can.

Rule #5: Have enough, but not too much, light! Remember that the quality of the image is better with a good light source. If possible, shoot outdoors only in daylight and let daylight into rooms. If you can't brighten up the room naturally, turn on more than one light. Remember that a strong, single light source will create shadows. To check the white balance on your camcorder, hold a piece of white paper right in front of the lens. Avoid backlighting (where the light source is behind your subject), or you may end up with only a silhouette.

White Balance: What color your camera "sees" as white

Rule #6: Pay attention to set-up! Do a test before you start. Film a bit (with sound) and use playback on your camcorder and earphones to make sure the sound and tape are recording correctly. One of my students once shot on location in another state and came home only to discover that the tape was unusable because the microphone wasn't connected properly. Save yourself the agony and do a test before filming!

Rule #7: Don't skimp! Shoot loads of footage! Shoot extra background footage and cutaways (extra shots from different angles). After you set up the shot the way you want it and make sure sound is recording properly, do the following:

- Press RECORD.
- Count to three (it takes that long for the camcorder to start recording).
- Cue the person who will be talking first.
- For stills, shoot for at least 10 or more seconds.
- If editing in-camera or assemble editing, add an extra few seconds to each clip.

Filming on Location

Filming on location is not very much different from the videotaped interview you may have already done. The same rules apply. Go over all the good rules for camera operations. Make sure you have a hand-held, unidirectional microphone attached to the camcorder.

If you are filming on private property, you will need to obtain permission from the owner. At national or other historic landmarks, you may need to contact those who are in charge ahead of time.

Try to set up the tripod and camera on even ground if possible. Although weather does not always cooperate, you would hope for a quiet, sunny day. If the location is near where you live, check it out ahead of time to see if the time of day you choose is relatively noise-free. You wouldn't want to film near a highway at rush hour, or by a school during recess or when it's time for buses to pick children up.

The person who is going to be the "on-camera talent" should be familiar with his or her lines, memorized if possible. If he or she has trouble memorizing, you may want to make large cue cards.

Watch out for monotone delivery! There is nothing worse than a flat, emotionless delivery of lines. The camera exaggerates everything because it focuses our attention completely on the subject. Make sure the on-camera talent is able to deliver the lines with some energy and without giggling.

Step 13

Editing

Linear Editing of Video

If you don't have access to computer editing software, it is possible to edit videotapes manually, although it is much more difficult. The difficulty here is that it is hard to jump back and forth between clips and be precise on starting and stopping.

If you intend to do linear editing, you must begin during the planning and production stages of your video. First of all, you would not be able to use digitized or scanned images in your documentary. If you have downloaded something from the Internet or scanned something from a book, you would need to print these out and film them with your camcorder. Likewise, all of your still shots would have to be filmed. You must film in the order of your storyboard so that you will have to edit the final product as little as possible.

To film in order (this is sometimes called *in-camera editing*), run a bit of blank tape at the very beginning. Of course, the first shot you will film will be your title. You will have prepared this on a printed sheet or even (*Very neatly, please!*) prepared it artistically by hand. Tape it to a wall and begin recording with your camcorder. Count out at least nine seconds, then stop recording. The usual length you would want a still on-camera would be six or seven seconds. This would give the viewer enough time to absorb the information. Of course, if there is a lot of writing or detail, you may want to go a couple of seconds longer. You will record two or three seconds longer than what you need in order to give yourself editing room.

To film your stills, you must time the narration to go with each one before filming. This way, you will know how long you must record each still. For the first still after the title (and every successive still), you must back up the tape in the camcorder by a tiny bit (this is why you filmed the two to three extra seconds). You want to begin recording over the top of what you ended with on the last record to eliminate any glitches or "snow" that may show up when viewing the tape. Record for as long as the narration will be for that still, plus another two seconds (back-up room).

This is a very difficult procedure and takes some skill. It is crucial to remember that, when you hit RECORD on the camcorder, there is a lag-time of about two or three seconds until the camera actually starts working. This amount of time is different for each camcorder. Practice a couple of shots, timing the taping process and then timing what has actually been recorded so you know how long your camera takes to actually start recording.

Adding in footage from professional documentaries or other primary source footage is more difficult. To do this, you would have to use a VCR and your camcorder (or two VCRs) to edit. This is called *assemble linear editing*.

To edit in this way, connect the output of your camcorder to the input of the VCR using audio and visual cables. Make sure the Video Out and Audio Out jacks on the camcorder are connected to the Video In and Audio In jacks on the VCR. Set the VCR to "Line Input" so that it is not recording from any other source.

The next thing you will do is to line up your positions. On your camcorder, put in your tape with your stills. Put a blank VHS tape in your VCR. Begin from your title screen. Hit RECORD on the VCR and PLAY on your camcorder. Play to a couple of seconds before the next position at which you need to do an insert. Hit STOP on your VCR. Again, you'll have to play with this to find out how much of a lag time there is between hitting PAUSE or STOP and the time your VCR actually stops recording. Take out the tape with the stills and put in your next source tape. Line it up to a second or two before you want to begin recording. Back up a second on your VCR to eliminate any static between scenes. Repeat the process above.

After your master tape has been created, you will need to put the narration in (if you did not read narration while filming stills). To do this, you will need a camcorder with an audio dub capability. Put the tape back in the camcorder and line up to the still. (You may want to practice reading the narration with the stills a couple of times before you do this). Hit "Audio Dub" and read the recording, pressing "Pause" on completion of each clip's narration. Play background music as you are recording because you will not have the option for a second sound track.

Edit Controllers

To make linear editing easier, there is a device called an edit controller. This is a machine that makes it possible to control the recording/stopping process during editing. With an edit controller, you "mark" each scene that will be in your final movie by pressing a button on the controller for starting and ending points. After you have marked all the scenes, you put a blank tape in your VCR, a source tape in your camcorder, start recording, and then pause. Push a button on the controller and it will take you to all the scenes on that tape. It takes over automatically, filming all the scenes on the tape in the order you want them to appear. Of course, this would mean you would have to have all footage on the same source tape, but that should not be difficult. Some controllers also give options for transition effects and titling.

Nonlinear or Desktop Editing

At this point, you will learn how to use computer editing software. This section will give you some of the basic principles, but will not

Nonlinear Editing: Not edited in order of filming. Able to edit clips randomly and rearrange them at will.

instruct you on any particular type of hardware and software. There is further advice in the "Technology Support" section of this book.

There are many different editing hardware and software programs on the market, but they all work in a similar way. In order to edit video on computer, you need (a) an input/output video capture card on the computer and/or firewire technology; and (b) editing software.

Input (capture) from video/output to videotape: Newer computers may have **firewire (IEEE P1394) technology,** which allows you to move video that has been filmed on a **digital camcorder** straight into the computer for editing and then output back to the digital camera for recording. A firewire does not let you capture on your computer video footage that has been shot on an **analog camcorder** or video from a standard VHS tape. To do this, you must have an analog video capture device that also lets you send analog output to a VCR.

Analog refers to the type of signal in which the information is encoded. Ordinary VHS tapes and TV broadcasting are analog, as opposed to the newer digital technology.

Editing software allows you to take the video that has been captured by your video graphics hardware and alter it for your needs. The best type of editing software programs allow you to integrate stills that have been shot with a digital camera, scanned, or saved from the Internet. The software should also allow you to add background music, along with narration and titles.

Editing on computer is really three separate processes: **Bringing in the information (importing or capturing)**; **editing and refining** by moving clips to their positions and adding elements like sounds, transitions, and captions/titles; and **publishing** your finished work to a VHS tape.

Bringing in Information

The first thing you need to do is realize that your computer can *import* graphics, MPEG (digitized video), and sound into the software program, just like you can import a picture into a word-processing document. You can also "capture" either digital or analog video and/or audio through the use of the video capture device (hardware that is installed on the computer).

Capturing Video

Each clip is entered separately to make it easier to edit your documentary.

- First, make sure your cables are connected correctly. Check the manual for the video capture card.
- Second, put the VHS tape from which you wish to import in a VCR and cue the VHS tape to just before (by a couple of seconds) the logged-in number count of your clip. (Use the same VCR that you used when you logged the clip.)
- Third, start your software program and begin a new file or enter one you've already started.
- Fourth, push PLAY on the VCR and hit the RECORD or CAPTURE feature of your software.
- Fifth, hit STOP on your software when you have finished capturing your shot, and hit STOP on the VCR.
- Sixth, play it back to make sure you didn't cut off the beginning or end of your clip. If you make a mistake, delete the clip and record it again. *Always delete the clip if you have made a mistake so that you save precious storage space on the hard drive!*

Importing or Recording Sound

Click on the SOUND tab or button within your software program. It should give you a feature to record narration. You will need to make sure your computer's microphone and record feature has been turned on. Record the narration for each shot separately, leaving a second of silence at the beginning and end of the narration. Speak slowly, paying careful attention to pronunciation. Don't use a monotone voice—put emphasis and feeling into the words. After recording, play the narration back, making sure that you have not been cut off at the beginning or end of the clip. If your software program lets you give sound clips a name, do so, or note what number the software gave it. Make a note on the script about the title under which the sound has been saved. This will help you to find the appropriate sound in the library when it is time to mix the sound with the graphic. Import other sound effects and music clips as needed.

Importing Graphics

By now, you have already scanned photos, saved them from Internet, or saved them from a digital camera. These photos must now be imported into your editing software. Hit the IMPORT button or tab in the editing software, search the hard drive (or floppy disc) for the graphic you wish to import, and then click OKAY. The graphic should show up in the editing software library, ready to be put into your video as a clip of whatever time duration you specify. (See the software manual for specifics on changing the length of time of clips.) Editing programs have different ways of representing the work in progress. Some programs offer a storyboard visual that shows thumbnails of visual images. To edit or change the order, you simply grab and drag. Other programs give a timeline option that shows you all the different elements of the video at once. You will see a line for visuals, one for narration, another for background music, and yet another for titling and special effects. This option lets you fine-tune and coordinate the elements of the video.

Editing

Editing is very simple once all of your video clips, sound bytes, and graphics have been entered. Most programs require you to simply grab the video clip or picture out of the program's library and place it in the appropriate spot on the storyboard line. You can use the program's editing features to adjust contrast, brightness, and length of visual. If the image looks blurry or distorted, see if the program gives you a "center in frame" option. If the image is still blurry, you may not be able to use it. There's an old saying that is especially true about graphic images: "Garbage in, garbage out." If the graphic was not saved in a good format or resolution, there is little you can do to correct the situation. When you have all the visuals in the order you wish them to appear, mix the sound with the visual. Make sure the time duration on the graphic is the right length for the sound. Shorten or lengthen the clips as needed.

Once you have all of your clips and your narration the way you want them, begin working on special effects like transitions and titles. A *transition* (when speaking about video) is a movement that occurs between your shots. An example is when the new shot comes in from the right and pushes the old shot out of the way, or you might see the swiping of the image (as if it were a clock), replacing the old shot with a new one. There are many different transition effects offered by programs. The usual one is the standard cut, which simply switches cleanly from one shot to another. Use special effects transitions sparingly. You should probably only use a special effect when you are switching from one subtopic to another. Use the clock-swipe transition to show the passage of time, for example, when your script jumps forward in time. Another special effect would be the rolling in of credits or a title screen.

Titles can be added to your video by typing in the text in the title portion of the software. This is very important because you will need an opening title screen, as well as a credits screen, in your video. You will also need to identify the speaker in any interview clips and sources for any clips you took from professional documentaries. The credits screen should give credit to any individuals who were interviewed on camera or who are helpful in supplying information or visuals. Organizations that gave you access to information, photographs, video clips, or sound should be cited. Any video production from which you captured footage should be cited. Music should also be cited.

Speaking of music, this is probably the last thing you will add to your video. See the page on "Choosing Music" included in Step 12. Once you have decided on appropriate music, it is easy to add it to the completed video by using the IMPORT button and recording from the CD-ROM. Add the music to sections of the video that you want to emphasize. Don't be afraid of silence! Sometimes eliminating music in crucial places can build tension and energy in the video.

Publishing to VHS Tape

Most software programs require you to "render" the movie before it can be printed to VHS tape. This can be done at the click of a button in the program, but it sometimes takes hours for the video to be rendered.

What occurs during this step is that the special effects, audio, and video elements are integrated together and compressed.

When rendering is done, you are ready to publish to tape. Make sure cables go out from computer and into the VCR according to directions for your video capture card. Make sure your movie is in the viewscreen and has been prepared by the computer. Push RECORD on the VCR, then click BEGIN or OUT TO VCR on your software. Let the entire movie play through, then push STOP on the VCR. Play back the movie and watch for any flaws or errors.

If you notice a glitch, it could be that your software is not linking correctly with your computer's video card. Go back to your movie and eliminate any tricky transitions. Try again. If you are still having trouble, refer to your software or hardware manual.

You can make as many copies of the documentary as allowed under "fair use" provisions of copyright law. Usually, this means two copies plus a master, in addition to one copy for each of the creators of the documentary.

Congratulations! You have produced your first documentary.

Step 14

Bibliography and Process Paper

The last step is to prepare your bibliography. If you are entering a competition, you will probably also need what is called a "process paper." This is a description of the process you went through during research and creation of your documentary and is usually limited to 500 words or less.

The title page should include the following information, neatly placed and centered on page:

- Title of Entry
- Students' name(s)
- Name of the contest
- Category (type of product)
- Division (Junior or Senior)

If you are entering a competition, you *may not* place information about what school you came from here or you may be disqualified from judging.

The process paper is a written (word-processed) description of the ways in which you researched and developed your product. This report includes some specific types of information, although each process paper will be a bit different. All papers must have some type of an introduction, research description, and conclusion. Usually, this covers some or all of the following information:

101

Introduction
- What the entry is about and a thesis statement.
- How you got your idea for the topic and how it relates to the theme (theme information could be placed in the conclusion instead, if you prefer).

Description of Research
- Where did you find your sources?
- What research leads did you pursue?
- What were your most valuable source(s)?
- How did your ideas change as you researched?
- What original thinking about the topic did you come up with?
- How did you put your entry together? What skills did you learn?
- What were some problems you overcame?

Conclusion
- Why is the topic important to study?
- How did the topic change history?
- What conclusions have you drawn?
- How has this been a valuable learning experience?

Your bibliography must be separated into primary and secondary sources and follow the style guide (MLA or Turabian's). An example is included in the "Organize, organize, organize" section of this handbook. List alphabetically under primary and secondary subtopics.

Some more hints: Make sure you print on only one side of a page. Double-spacing is not necessary, and single spacing is usually preferable. Staple the document in the upper left-hand corner. Do not use binders or any other cover.

Student Self-Assessment

Now, it is time to celebrate everything you have learned. It is important to complete this step so that you can appreciate your hard work.

Step One: Skills You Have Learned
Place a check next to each skill that you have acquired during your research and production process.

_____ note taking	_____ research	_____ organization	_____ bibliography
_____ oral interview	_____ telephone work	_____ letter-writing	_____ library catalogues
_____ Internet	_____ scanning	_____ digital camera	_____ work a camcorder
_____ topic knowledge	_____ map reading	_____ surveys	_____ graphs/charts
_____ oral presentation	_____ word processing	_____ computer editing	_____ camera skills
_____ writing	_____ problem solving	_____ analysis	_____ storyboarding

Step Two: Analyze Your Final Product
Answer the following questions by checking the appropriate column

In your documentary, did you . . .	Most of Time	Sometimes	Rarely
Support your main ideas with accurate historical facts?			
Demonstrate and prove your own viewpoint?			
Have an original interpretation and thoughtful analysis?			
Establish the time period and context of your topic?			
Acknowledge other points of view?			
Establish cause-and-effect relationships?			
Use primary sources whenever possible?			
Organize the media so that they are easily understood?			
Establish a timeline of events?			
Use enough graphic images to get your point across?			
Use primary source footage?			
Use interviews?			
Use music or other sound to communicate emotion?			
Narrate with feeling and emphasis?			
Narrate with an even tone and volume of voice?			
Use transitions between scenes?			
Have background music when appropriate?			
Use good quality camera techniques? (i.e. zoom, tilt, pan, holding steady, etc.)			
Use close-ups and vary shots to emphasize points?			
Have a credits screen?			
Have a title screen that created an impact?			
Have a neatly written, well-organized bibliography?			

About the Author

Deborah Escobar is a teacher of the gifted and talented in New York State. She has a bachelor's degree in social studies/secondary education from Russell Sage College and a master's degree from University of the State of New York at Albany. She has served as a judge for the National History Day program for the past eight years, and her students frequently rise to the national level of History Day. In 1992, Deborah was named a Sally Mae Outstanding New Teacher of the Year, and in 2001 she was named New York State History Day Teacher of the Year. She is an expert on using primary sources and technology in the classroom and has been the recipient of many state grants to develop teaching materials that incorporate their use. She has taught "Creating Documentaries," a teacher in-service course offered by the New York State Historical Association, and she has also created video documentaries for community groups, including one that led to a public effort to raise restoration funds for a one-room schoolhouse.